Liturgy

J. McDaniel

LITURGY AND ARCHITECTURE

LOUIS BOUYER
of the Oratory

LITURGY and ARCHITECTURE

University of Notre Dame Press: 1967

Library of Congress Catalog Card Number 67-25644
Manufactured in the United States of America

CONTENTS

I.	The Ancient Synagogues	8
II.	The Early Syrian Churches	24
III.	The Roman Basilicas	39
IV.	The Byzantine Churches	60
V.	The Western Churches	70
VI.	Tradition and Renewal	86
Appendix I: Concelebration		120
Appendix II: The Baptistry		121
Index		123

ILLUSTRATIONS

1	Style of the very early synagogues	18
2	Location of the altar in the early Syrian church	26
3	Location of the altar in the Roman basilica-type church	47
4	Location of the altar in the early Byzantine church	64
5	Eastern arrangement in Western churches	73
6	Central or western choir arrangement in Western churches	78
7, 8, 9	Ideal arrangements suggested for modern churches	99
10	Further possibilities of choir arrangements	102
11	Altar facing the people located in the nave of the church	113

LITURGY and ARCHITECTURE

IN THE CONSTITUTION ON THE LITURGY, the Fathers have insisted that liturgical renewal is much more than a matter of new rubrics. Even the best material changes in this field, such as a wider extension of the vernacular or fuller use of Scripture, would remain meaningless if not accompanied by a change in the spirit in which we are to perform the liturgy.

"Spirit," in the Christian sense of the word, does not mean just a purely interior feeling or idea. It means that, certainly, but it involves much more. "Spirit" always means, for Christians, some interior reality, one which tends toward incarnation, or rather cannot even exist without being incarnate. It is not just in the rubrics that the spirit of the liturgy has to take flesh, whatever may be their use and even necessity in leading us along the right path. It is in a general behavior, in a whole atmosphere, more deeply, it is in what we call an "ethos," a turn of mind and heart which is to pervade all the details of the ritual, so as to make of them all a coherent embodiment of that "spirit" which is not just the spirit of man, but what this becomes when the Holy Spirit, the Spirit of God, is at work in man.

How then can we define the spiritual renewal which has to take place not only in the liturgical field, there, perhaps, first of all and above all, since the same Constitution makes it so clear that the liturgy is at the heart of the whole life of the Church: that to which everything is tending, or from which everything results? We could sum it up by saying that we are to recover the true sense and reality of tradition.

For the last centuries, with the "siege" mentality of the Church of the Counter-Reformation, hardening itself to resist external attacks or temptations, there has been an unconscious or subconscious tendency to reduce tradition to a merely external handing of some practices and formulae, to be kept unchanged in their materiality, with little or no attention paid to their meaning. This was a dangerously distorted view of Christian tradition. It is not surprising therefore if we see now a counter-tendency to discard tradition understood in that way, in order to regain a Christianity fully alive. But if we were, as a consequence, to discard tradition altogether, far from reviving true Christianity, we should just throw it overboard.

For Christianity, authentic Christianity, lives only by tradition, not a tradition of dead formulae or mechanical practices, but a tradition of life, a life that is to grow organically, in and through some embodiment. In the continuity of that body, as well as in its ever renewed aspects, both the permanence and the ever creative power of the same Spirit have to be constantly manifested and exercised.

To descend to concrete reality, the liturgy is the life of prayer and worship of a single community, the mystical Body of Christ, developing through history, from a certain unique source, the teaching and the saving action of Our Lord, ever active in us through the Holy Spirit. We are to be taken into the life of that Body of Christ, of that community of believers which is above all the community of the Spirit.

We are, therefore, to receive from the past

the forms of prayer and worship, but not a dead past. It is a legacy of life. It has, first, to be fully recognized as such, in the documents of the past, in order to remain ever fruitful and active, and if need be creative, in the present and for the future.

As soon as we begin to look at the liturgical monuments of the past in that light, we can realize the immense richness and vast amount of freedom that the Catholic tradition puts at our disposal. The better we know and understand, as from inside, the creative power of the Spirit which has manifested itself in the liturgical forms we have inherited, the more quickly we discover that, far from having to break with the tradition to answer the needs of our own times, it is by rediscovering its plenitude that we shall be both free and able to do so. Always presupposing that we look at the liturgical forms not as they may have become, when they were not any more understood and had ceased to be the object of an intelligent, active and fruitful participation on the part of the faithful (as the Council says again and again), but as they were in their original freshness.

The liturgy then will appear to us as what it is: a common life in the Spirit, a common life of God with men, through the experience of which men become one together, while becoming one with God in Christ.

And here it is that the architecture comes in. For the liturgy is nothing else, but the gathering together of mankind in the house of the Father. It is that marriage feast of the Lamb where all are called, to be reconciled in the Body of the only Son, at the same time with the Father and between themselves. Here all the scattered children are to congregate and to be made at last one in the Bride of the Lamb, the Church.

Of course, as Christians, it is true in a sense that we can have no other permanent dwelling but a heavenly House. But this celestial mansion has to be built out of the living stones which we are to become, so that the eternal Temple of the heavenly God, on the corner stone of Christ, rises on earth, in our own time. This is what happens when we meet together, to hear God's word, to answer His word in prayer, and to become united with Him and among ourselves by the sacramental celebration of the mystery proclaimed by His word: that mystery which is, as Saint Paul has it, "Christ in us, the hope of our glory."

The places where we do that, although they are only transitory tabernacles on the way of our pilgrimage toward the heavenly Temple, are to provide as it were the visible frame of the Church, and, insofar, are rightly called "churches." They are, here on earth, true houses of God with His people. Their functional adaptation to the making in time of the one true and everlasting Church is a basic expression on earth of what we are to do there which, however imperfect it may be, is a preparation for and even some inauguration of, what we are to do in future eternity.

Where is the spirit of men more apparent than in the homes that they build to house their lives? In the same manner, it is the way in which we shall build our churches which will be a manifestation par excellence of the kind of Church life, of common life in the Body of Christ, that will be ours.

It must be acknowledged that to-day what most of our churches reveal is not very inspired or inspiring. Most of the time they are still a routine reproduction of models of the past imperfectly or not at all understood. Copied from outside, they do not seem to have been made to embody a life springing up from inside the community they are to house.

Even when we try to be "modern" we too often only adapt to the use of the Church some kind of modern building, a civic assembly hall, a big class-room, or a cinema, trying to furnish it with a few features picked up from the old routine building, supposedly more "traditional." Neither way can do. We must look elsewhere if we want a place where Christian worship will come to life again, and not just be fossilized in an outworn shell or crushed on some Procrustean bed. The only possible way is first to try to rediscover how the Christian liturgy, at the most creative period of its existence, remodelled the older buildings it had used in the beginning and then evolved out of them something quite new. When we have done that we may hope to find the inspiration we need to do the same for our own times, in the same Spirit of the Christianity of all times, and in accordance with other circumstances, offering new possibilities.

When we look at the churches which were arranged or built on purpose to house the Christian liturgy at the height of its freshness and creative power, we see that it is not a series of fixed details, all taken in isolation or together, which is important. It is rather a dynamic relation between some different focuses of the celebration, embodied in various elements and their coherent disposition. This may give, and has given, rise to an almost unlimited variety of patterns. But all of these patterns become dead as soon as they are copied materially, without the right understanding of what gave them their sense. Only an historical approach can give the clue of their genesis: then we see how it is the vital function alone which can explain the organ, and not the dead organ which will ever provide a misunderstood or forgotten function.

I. THE ANCIENT SYNAGOGUES

The Church, whether we mean by this name the Body of Christ of which we are members or the building where it is to meet, has not been created ex nihilo at the coming of Christ. The New Testament was born not only out of the Old but from it. Contemporary exegesis has underlined how the Church, as the Body of Christ, had its preparation in the Qahal, the assembly of the People of God, brought together to hear the word, to surrender to it in common prayer, to be sealed in the unity of the Covenant, an alliance with God. And the Church, the material temple in which this assembly of God is to meet, when He Himself becomes the link with His own, had its immediate preparation in the Jewish synagogue.[1]

It is sometimes supposed that the synagogue itself differed from the older Temple of Jerusalem because it was just a place for teaching: a school of the holy word. That the importance of teaching and meditating together the word of God became paramount in the synagogue is certainly true. But modern scholarship, especially the researches of the Scandinavian scholars, has demonstrated the fallacy of opposing the religion of the synagogue as a religion of the word to the religion of the Temple as a ritual religion. It has shown that the origin of the religion of the word was in the ritual religion of Israel, the religion of the Temple itself, and, before the Temple existed, the religion of the other sanctuaries, to which the guilds of prophets were attached from the beginning. Reciprocally whatever may have been the importance of reading God's word in the synagogal worship, the synagogue has never become just a kind of reli-

[1] Cf. E. L. SuKENIK, *Ancient Synagogues in Palestine and Greece,* London, 1934.

gious school-room. For the teaching of the own. And this was the Presence which, for the much more than "teaching," in the ordinary use of the term. It was a matter of the whole life of the people, a true encounter with God, a renewed consecration to His alliance or covenant. Therefore the synagogal worship was included and has never ceased to be included in a ritual celebration, closely connected with the acknowledgement and the cult of a special Presence of God with His own. And this was the Presence which for the Jews, has always been connected with the Temple or the place where it stood, more especially the Holy of holies where the God that the heavens cannot house has nevertheless condescended to dwell in the midst of His own.

The synagogal worship was therefore organized around two focuses, the relation between which reveals its spiritual dynamism. Whatever may have been the varied disposition of the ancient synagogues, we find that it gravitates around them, always in the same manner.

In the midst of the synagogue there was always "the seat of Moses." This phrase, indeed, which we find in the Gospels on the lips of Our Lord, was not just a metaphor to describe the teaching of the scribes. The *sunagoge,* that is the *qahal,* the assembly of the People of God could meet as such only because there was always among them some one held as the authentic depositary of the living tradition of God's word, first given to Moses, and able to communicate it always anew, although always substantially the same. This then, at the time of Our Lord, was the proper function of the rabbis as the "Doctors in Israel." The assembly was grouped around a ceremonial seat which was considered the seat of Moses, the seat from which the word embedded in a tradition still alive, could be received.

That tradition was not just a human tradition but the tradition of the people of God and the word of God, was made clear by the first focus of the synagogue: the Ark.

In a way, the seat already could be looked upon as a focus of the meeting. But it was not an autonomous focus. Its importance was only derivative. The rabbi himself, as everybody else in the synagogue, looked toward the Ark.

What was the Ark in the Old Testament? It is not easy to give a precise answer, except that the Ark was the most holy thing of the old covenant, so holy indeed that it was the only object which had ever been admitted in the Holy of holies, the *debir* of the Temple. We have in the first book of Kings, the history of the well meaning Oziah who, while the Ark was being brought to Jerusalem, extended his hand to prevent it from falling from the chariot on which it had been set, and who was struck dead on the spot for that apparently innocent familiarity.

Materially, the Ark of the Tabernacle and of the Temple was a kind of wooden casket. It has indeed been supposed that its form had been suggested by the Egyptian casket of Osiris, a coffin, but this is doubtful for it is clear that, although the Ark was used as a repository for holy things, first of all the tables of the Law, the "testimony" given to Moses, it was not so much its inside that attracted the attention as the empty space above it. The ark, in fact, was understood as a throne, an empty throne where nothing, especially no graven image, was to be seen. On this throne, God Himself was supposed to be present, the sole object of the worship of Israel.

On both sides therefore, the Cherubim, that is a representation of the elementary spirits, *ta stoicheia tou kosmou,* as Saint Paul would say, the object themselves of the misguided adoration of the other peoples were to be seen. But they were there in adoration before the awful presence, which their wings reverently protected from any profane approach, together with the veil hiding the ark. "Thou who sittest between the cherubim" was the usual invocation to the heavenly God as having condescended, in His grace and love toward His people to freely take His abode among them.

This localised presence in the Temple, in the Holy of holies on the cover of the ark, between the Cherubim, was called by the rabbis the Shekinah. The word means the presence under the tent, the tabernacling presence of the almighty God as a sojourner among His own. The cloud of light which had filled first the Tabernacle and later the Temple of Solomon when both had been erected, was its hidden manifestation. From that presence between the Cherubim, God had been supposed to speak to Moses and Aaron, afterwards to Samuel. At a much later period the calling of Isaiah will take the form of a vision in the Temple, of that same presence environed not only by the visible Cherubim but also by the Seraphim, the spirits of fire that heavenly fire of the Pillar of the cloud and of the Sinai, singing the ritual hymn of adoration of the *Shekinah;* "Holy, holy, holy the Lord God Sabaoth: the earth is full of His glory!"

And when Ezekiel will describe God leaving His Temple, polluted by idolatry before it is abandoned to the Gentiles, he will show the presence on the *Merkabah,* the chariot of fire of the Ophanim taking its flight from the Mount Sion, invisibly to accompany the faithful remnant into exile.

In fact the Ark of the Temple had disappeared at the time of the exile. Even when the Temple would have been rebuilt, it would never be found or replaced. The Holy of holies, thenceforth, would remain absolutely empty.

The Ark of the synagogues remains as an echo of the primitive Ark, on the cover of which year after year, the blood of the atonement had been sprinkled as a token of reconciliation between God and the people. Its link with the one authentic and irrecoverable ark was the presence in it of the scrolls of the Torah, just as the token of God's presence had been the Tables of the Decalogue in the former one.

Just as in the Holy of holies, the Ark of every synagogue was protected by a veil, in front of which burned the seven lamps of the *Menorah,* the seven-branched candlestick.

Nevertheless, as there was everywhere one and the same Torah, no synagogue could be as it were, self-centered. The Ark, in all of them, still pointed to something beyond itself. And this was the ultimate focus of the synagogal worship: the Holy of holies, the one and only *debir* at Jerusalem. Now it was empty of the former ark. Later it would even be utterly destroyed. For the Jews of the diaspora, it did not for all that, cease to be the only place where God finally had willed His Name to be present, and, insofar, Himself. Thus have all the synagogues, at the time of Our Lord and since that time, been oriented. And their orientation is precisely toward Jerusalem, more specifically toward what remains, for the Jews, the sacred place par excellence: the site of the Holy of holies.

Another feature of all the synagogues was the place from which both the Torah (with the Prophets) and the prayers were to be read. The sacred books could be read publicly not only by the rabbi or any one of the elders who had their seats on benches around him, but by any member of the community. The prayers were said either by the Cantor or Minister, as it is the case to-day, or by a member of the community able to act as its *sheliah sibbur,* its representative (literally: its apostle). That place, in Greek-speaking times came to be called the *bema.* It was a platform in a central position so that the reader might be heard by everybody and to which was later adapted a lectern.

Although, in early synagogues, there may have been some distance between the *bema,* the seat of Moses and the benches for the elders, there was an early tendency to bring them together. We can infer that such was the case in the synagogue of Nazareth, where Saint Luke says that Our Lord, having returned to the minister the scroll from which He had read Isaiah 61, sat down as the rabbis did, to preach.

At the time when the Mishnah was finally compiled, the seats could even be on the side of the *bema* where the ark was, as is now the case, since it is said that the elders, seated so as to face the congregation, turned to the back of their seats to pray toward Jerusalem. However, this does not seem to have been the prevailing custom in the first centuries of our era. When we have some positive indication of its situation, the seat of Moses appears to have been rather on the other side, sometimes at the end of the room, more generally nearer the center.

Very early, the Jews made use for their synagogues, of the typical Greek building for public meetings: the basilica. It was quadrilateral in shape, with two rows of columns, leaving two aisles free for the movements of those entering. There were one or three doors, usually, at one end, sometimes on one side. In the oldest synagogues of that type, the doors are always facing in the direction of Jerusalem. The result of this was that the Ark blocked the central door especially when, from being a wooden casket, it was further elaborated into a small building of masonry. From that time (in the second or third century of our era) the basilica building was used in the opposite direction. It was not any longer the main door but the wall opposite it which indicated the direction of Jerusalem, and, finally, the Ark came to be located in an apse at this end, and the bema together with the seats were brought to the same end.

Whatever might have been the respective disposition of the furniture, we find always the same relation between the congregation,

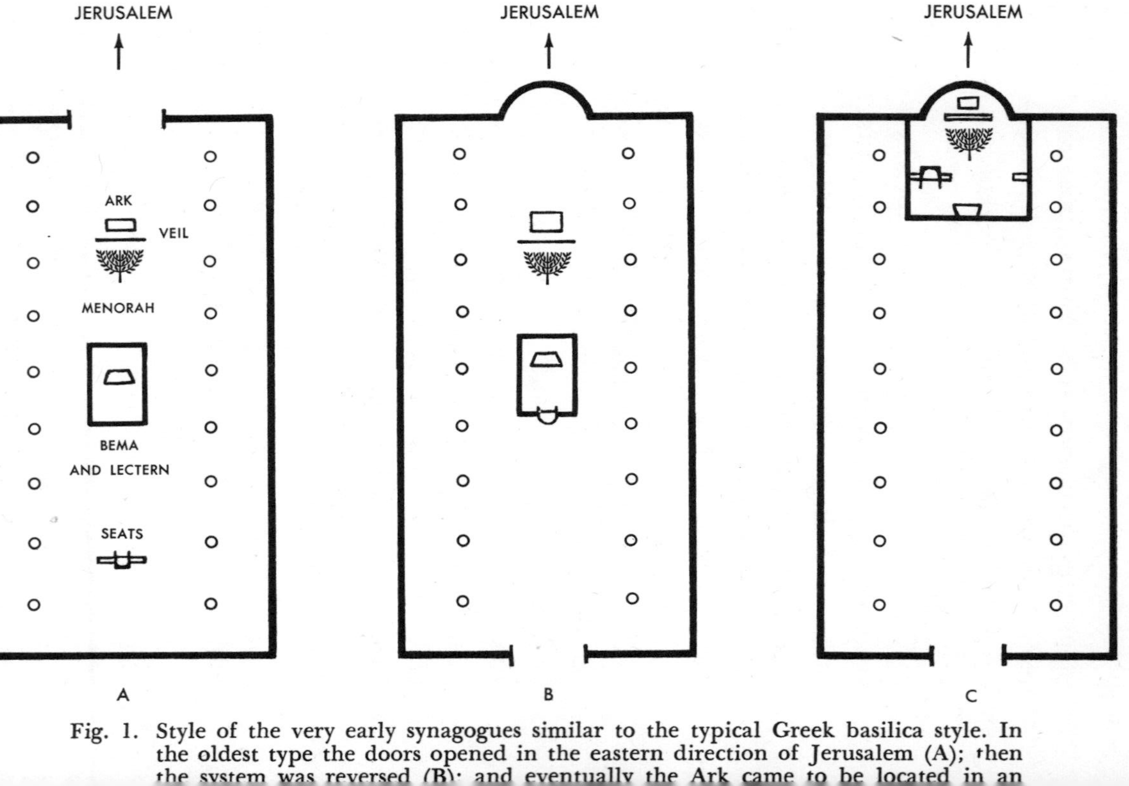

Fig. 1. Style of the very early synagogues similar to the typical Greek basilica style. In the oldest type the doors opened in the eastern direction of Jerusalem (A); then the system was reversed (B); and eventually the Ark came to be located in an

grouped around the seat of Moses, the Ark and Jerusalem. The congregation gathered around the rabbi and his teaching. But the ark, from which were produced the scrolls of the Law and the Prophets, remained for all the focus of the continued presence of God, where the faithful remnant was brought together to meditate upon the Torah. However, beyond the ark itself, the prayers of the People were still directed toward the Holy of holies of Jerusalem, to the place where the Messiah was to appear and the diaspora to be gathered ultimately in a rebuilt Jerusalem.

Thus we see how the cult of the synagogue, in spite of the centrality of reading and meditating the word of God, was not just "teaching," in the ordinary sense of the word. It was teaching, certainly, but teaching of a word understood as the word of life, in which God committed Himself, communicated Himself to His people, so as to become present in the midst of them. And that presence could not be reduced to a moral influence in the ethical life of the community. It included that. But it implied much more. If ritual religion became moralized in that form of worship, as it was indeed, it can be said no less truly, even more truly, that ethics, morality, in its turn, was sacralized. And this sacrality itself was expressed in a ritual or sacramental factor, which, until now, in orthodox Judaism, has remained uppermost: the localized presence, by grace and love, of the transcendent God in the sanctuary of Jerusalem, the Holy of holies.

Even after the destruction of the Temple, the Jews in the synagogues will continue to pray facing Jerusalem, facing what was formerly the place of the *debir*. And this is not just a persistent attachment to the past, a clinging to some historical manifestation of God which has now ceased for ever. In their view, it is much more an expectation of the future. The place of the Temple, the vestiges of it remain sacred because the divine Shekinah will return there at the coming of the Messiah. Then the Temple once again will be restored and a reconstructed Jerusalem will be a lasting home for a gathering of the whole diaspora into one People, nevermore to be scattered among the *goyim*.

In the interim, however, this is not only prefigured but prepared for in the invisible but real presence of the Shekinah with the faithful remnant, according to the promise of Ezekiel, at the time of the first exile and dispersion. Where is that interim presence to be found? Everywhere and when ten Jews are gathered together to hear and meditate upon the Torah, say the rabbis. And that gives to the synagogal service, centered upon the reading of the Torah, a ritual character which amounts to a quasi-sacramental and sacrificial reality. Hence the ritual features centered on the Ark: the *Menorah* and the veil, together with the relation between the Ark and the Holy place manifested in the orientation of the Ark on the axis of Jerusalem. Hence also the fact that the prayers connected with the unfolding and the reading of the scrolls kept in the ark will both be evolved out of ritual prayers, originally connected with the performance of the sacrifices in the Temple, and become accepted by the rabbis as a present equivalent of these sacrifices.

The first of the two great prayers of the synagogal ritual, the series of the three *berakoth* leading to the recitation of the *Shemah,* will culminate in the saying together of the *Kedushah,* the hymn of the Seraphim in Isaiah 6, and the *berakah* for the sacred presence, the hymn of the Cherubim and the Ophanim in Ezekiel 3. Odeberg has suggested that these hymns originally in the synagogal worship itself, were the summit of the cult, the *Shemah* (now considered as holding that place) having been introduced only later. He is probably wrong in thinking that of the synagogal worship itself. But the truth must be that the association of men with these heavenly canticles, in the worship of the Temple, had probably been a central feature of the offering of the sacrifice of incense, morning and evening of every day.

Similarly, the other great prayer of the synagogue, the *Tefillah* of the Eighteen Benedictions (now Nineteen) still culminates with the recitation of the *Abodah* which, according to the rabbis, was formerly the consecration prayer of the daily burnt offering in the Temple. To this prayer in the festivals of the Temple, even now celebrated in the synagogues, was and is still added an invocation that the "memorial" of the People, of the house of David, of the Messiah, arise, be heard accepted before God and come to pass, so that the Coming of the Messiah and the final restoration of Israel may happen. This "memorial," thus expressed in the Jewish liturgy, is evidently seen as the expression of the essence of the sacrificial worship.

We must even say more. The synagogal

worship, already before Christ, has had its necessary complement in the ritual of the meals: the family meal, and better still, at least at the time of Christ, the meals of those communities of faithful brought together by a common messianic expectation around a "Master of justice," like those of Qumran, Damascus, the Essenes and probably the Therapeutes described by Philo and Josephus.

In these meals these communities found not only an equivalent but a better substitute for the sacrifices of the Temple, and an immediate prefiguration and preparation for the coming of the messianic Kingdom. In the breaking of the bread, in the blessing of the cup of thanksgiving and their common participation, they saw an inauguration of the messianic feast. Soon this banquet would gather in a renewed Jerusalem the definitive People of God. In accordance with this view, the same sacrificial re-presentation of the "memorial," which was the conclusion of the prayer *Abodah* in the Temple for the consecration of the sacrifices of the great festivals, was also added to the last *berakah,* over the last cup.

Something of this home ritual has passed into the synagogal worship itself in the Christian era. It is the blessing of the *Kidush,* the cup of wine blessed and partaken among the worshippers on the eve of a festival.

But it would be the Christians who would introduce, as the conclusion of their synagogal worship itself, the "eucharistic" meal, as the new and definitive sacrifice, the expectation of the second *Parousia* of a Messiah already manifested in Jerusalem, and now expected to reign over the whole world.

II. THE EARLY SYRIAN CHURCHES

The most ancient type of a Christian Church seems to be that of the old Syrian churches.[2] It is known to us both through archaeological discoveries and through liturgical documents of Christian antiquity such as the *Apostolic Constitutions* and the Syriac *Didascalia apostolorum.* Moreover it has more or less survived until our own days in the Nestorian Churches. These, probably the most conservative, keep to this day traditions which, already at the time of the Fathers, were considered archaic. Much of the same traditions has also been retained in the Jaco-

[2] Cf., in the edition of Funk, *Didascalia Apostolorum,* II, s7, 3; vol. I. pp. 158–162, and *Constitutions Apostolorum,* II, 57, 3 ss; ibid., pp. 159–165.

bite Syrian Churches as well as among the Syrian Catholics.[3]

There we have the remnants of a primitive Christianity which, even when it had ceased to be purely Jewish, remained for a time purely semitic. It separated from the great Church, as it is now growingly recognized, at the time of the Nestorian or Monophysite controversies (in the fifth century), not so much for doctrinal motives as to safeguard those semitic traditions which were then felt to be endangered by the hellenization of the Byzantine Church in the Byzantine Empire.

Therefore, it is not surprising, that the old Syrian church appears as a Christianized version of a Jewish synagogue. Using, as contemporary synagogues, the basilica type of build-

[3] Cf. J. Lassus, *Sanctuaires chrêtiens de Syrie,* Paris, 1947 et "Liturgies nestoriennes meievales et eglises syriennes antiques," *Revue d'Histoire des Religions* (1950), pp. 236 ff.; J. Lassus and G. Tchalenko, "Ambons syriens," *Cahiers archeologiques,* V, 1951; J. Dauvillier, "L'ambon ou bema dans les textes de l'Eglise chaldeenne et de l'Eglise syrienne au moyen-age," *Cahiers archeologiques,* VI, 1952; Mme. N. Maurice-Denis Boulet, "L'autel dans l'antiquite chretienne, *La Maison-Dieu,* XXIX (1952); and above all: Dennis Hickley, *The Ambo in early liturgical planning,* in *The Heuthrop Journal,* October 1966, pp. 407 ss. On the problem of orientation and its Christian interpretation, see F. Dölger, *Sol salutis,* Münster, 1925 (2nd. ed.)

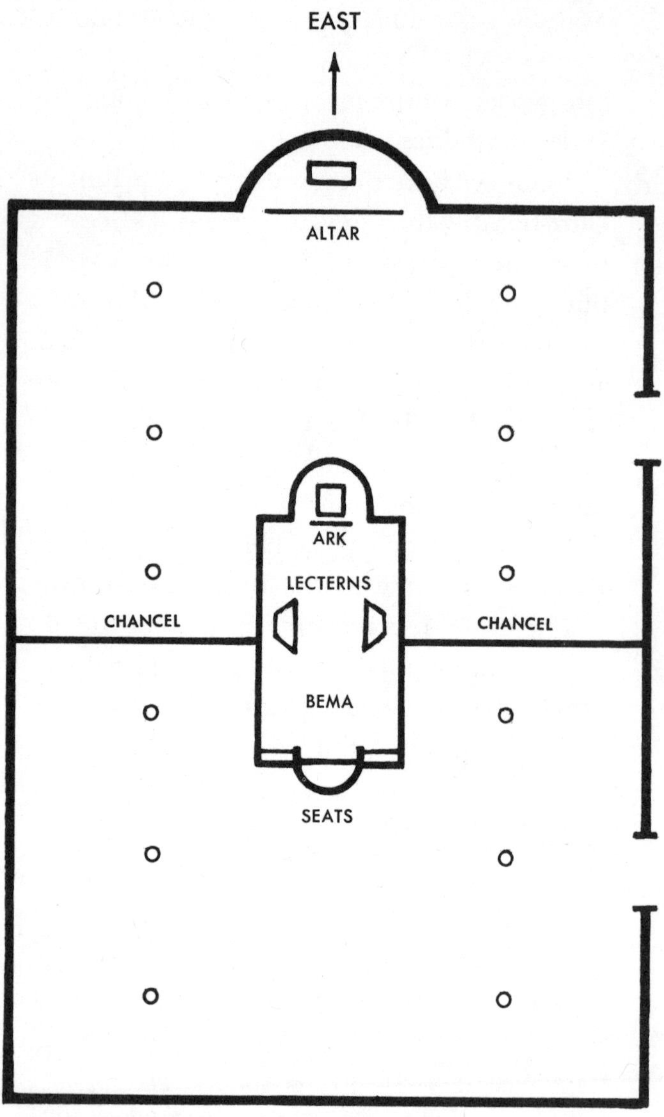

Fig. 2. Location of the altar in the early Syrian church pointing to the east, for these Christians not to Jerusalem but to the rising sun, the Sun of Justice.

ing, they appropriate it to worship in a similar way. We have, as in the synagogue, the office of readings and prayers everywhere performed on a *bema,* which regularly occupies the center of the nave. The Ark also is still there, between the *bema* and the apse, and it has kept both its veil and its candlestick. On the other side of the *bema,* the seat of the bishop has replaced what was formerly the seat of Moses, and the Christian presbyters sit around, as did the Jewish elders before them.

However, two differences are striking after we become aware of these similarities. One is that these churches are no longer oriented toward Jerusalem, the Holy of holies toward which the apse or closing wall of the synagogues was directed. Their apse is now directed toward the geographical east, the point where the sun actually rises. The other one is that the apse neither remains empty, as in the more ancient synagogues, nor receives the ark of scriptures, as in the more recent. It has become the location of a table, generally affecting a sigma shape (like our letter C), at a short distance from the wall. A second veil has been introduced, before that table, which is of course the Christian altar.

What does all that mean? The sense of both changes is obvious.

First, the earthly Jerusalem and its Holy of holies have lost their meaning for Christians. For them, not only the Temple does not exist any longer, but its place has definitely lost its former sacred association. The new Jerusalem they are expecting is not any reconstruction of the old one. It is a heavenly Jerusalem whose foundations are "above" and not in any place of this world. For them, indeed, as for the Jews, it is to appear at the coming of the Messiah. But in his second and final parousia, He will not bring back the Shekinah to where it was formerly. The heavenly city will be made of the gathering of the elect in His risen body, coming to its fulfilment in the Church of the last day. And in this city there will be no need of any Temple, for the Lord Himself, in His union with them, will be the eternal Temple.

Hence the orientation of the Christian churches. The East, as the place of the rising sun for the early Christians, was the only fitting symbol of the last appearance of Christ in His parousia, as that Sun of justice sung of already in the canticle of Zechariah. We may be inclined, to-day, to minimize the importance of that symbolism. But the whole of ancient Christian archaeology, together with the most ancient Christian literature, bears a unanimous witness to its importance for the first Christians. We can here only send back the reader to the monograph of Dölger, *Sol salutis,* and to the more recent studies of Professor Cyrille Vogel, on the fullness of meaning it had for them. Already Tertullian, in his treatise on prayer, supposes that it is an apostolic tradition to pray either publicly or privately always facing East.

In this symbolism was expressed the eschatological expectation of primitive Christianity: the expectation that is of a last day, the lasting day of eternity, in which the *Christus victor* would appear as the rising sun which will never set.

That this may have been felt even in Syria and Palestine where the Holy land was a concrete reality, is the sign of its decisive importance for the first Christians. At the time of Constantine, Jerusalem would be restored as a Christian city. The sites of Calvary, of the empty tomb, of the garden of Gethsemani and the Mount of Olives would be honored.

A new Jerusalem liturgy would develop, centered on the commemoration of the Gospel events at their (real or supposed) location. Then it could have been thought that a tendency should have arisen, perhaps, of again praying facing Jerusalem. But, even in Palestine, we discover nothing of this. In the whole Roman province of Syria (which included Palestine), after as before the restoration of Jerusalem as a holy and now Christian city, as everywhere else, the Christian will continue to pray, not toward Jerusalem but toward the East. The earthly Jerusalem, even when it has become a place of pilgrimage, and of the most popular one, will remain supplanted and absorbed, in the vision of the faithful, by that heavenly Jerusalem which is the Body of the Lord of glory, the eternal source of life and light.

All that, however, does not mean that for the first Christians there will not be a place on this earth also where the Shekinah, the divine presence with us, may be localized. But this place will be every place where the eucharist comes to be celebrated. There, indeed, some foretaste of the last day will be found in a mysterious coming of the heavenly Lord. For, in the eucharist, under the visible symbols of the bread and wine, a presence will be acknowledged by faith of the Body and Blood of the dead and risen Christ, intended to feed our hope of being found "in Him" at the last day.

Hence a third intermediary focus of the Christian celebration at the visible end of the oriented axis of the Christian church, near the Eastern wall or apse: the altar, the table of the eucharistic meal. The Jews in the synagogue, hearing the word of God, looked at the Ark and beyond the Ark at the Jerusalem Holy of holies which it evoked. The Christians in their churches, hearing the word, are led by it from the Ark to the altar. And beyond the altar itself, they look toward no other earthly place but only toward the rising sun as toward the symbol of the *Sol justitiae* they are expecting. The holy table, for them, is the only possible equivalent on earth of what was for the Jews their Holy of holies. In the Syrian churches this was manifested by the second veil hiding the altar added to that which still veiled the Ark, just as in the Temple of old, a first veil hid the holy place and a second one veiled the Holy of holies.

With its *anamnesis,* that is its memorial

represented every Sunday of the saving death of Christ in the expectation of the resurrection, which will extend to all the members of Christ on the last day, the eucharistic meal has taken the place of the former sacrifices. No other sacrifice can have now any meaning, but the cross of Christ celebrated in the Christian meal. Through it, while taking part in His passion, we are being given a foretaste of His resurrection.

The seat of the bishop, as the doctor of the apostolic tradition of the new covenant, has taken the place of the seat of Moses. It is the word of God still that creates the congregation of the faithful, the *Qahal* or Church of the New Testament as formerly of the Old. But now, it is that word having come to its definitive fullness in the Gospel of the Word made man. The most sacred scroll, therefore, in the ark is not any longer that of the Torah, but the book of the Gospels. The Gospel itself, to prepare us for the eternal gathering of the elect in the heavenly Jerusalem, leads us toward the expected Orient, whence its coming is hoped for, by inviting us to the messianic feast, the banquet of the Lamb, now already inaugurated in the eucharistic celebration. Here at last all the preparatory sacrifices have found their ultimate consummation: in the bloodless sacrifices of that Lamb who has been immolated once for all, and remains for ever interceding on our behalf in the immediate presence of the Father in the celestial Holy of holies, as our forerunner. And here on earth we partake of His resurrected Body. Already we drink the new life of His love by taking part of the cup of blessing, the chalice of His Blood.

In some places in Syria there will be a further modification of the disposition of these elements which is worth mentioning. First of all, the ark will be modified, so as to become more visibly the throne which it has always been understood to be, for the divine presence. There, at the beginning of every *synaxis,* of every liturgical assembly, the book of the Gospels will be solemnly enthroned. This may have been occasioned by the last great persecution under Diocletian, in which the pagan officials were especially requested to seize the Christian scriptures. Therefore they had to be kept habitually in some more secret place, from which they were to be taken only for use in public worship.

In some churches this throne will even take the place of the seat of Moses itself at the

Western end of the *bema.* Thus it will be made clear that the Christian bishop, or any preacher of the Gospel, is only the surrogate for Christ. This may have been the case especially in small churches where usually at the eucharist the bishop did not preside, but one of the presbyters. We know that at Antioch itself, at the time of the solution of the local schism in the fourth century, it was agreed that the two conflicting bishops would sit on both sides of the enthroned Gospel.

This however has never become the general practice. The typical Syrian church has remained to this day a church where the bishop (or the priest presiding at the celebration) sits at the Western end of the *bema,* in the middle of the clergy, while the Gospel is enthroned at the other end of it. Two lecterns, usually, accompany it, one on the southern side for the Gospel, the other on the northern side for the other readings.

After the service of scripture readings and prayers, all the clergy, taking with them the offerings of the faithful, go to the East, while the congregation reassembles itself around the altar for the eucharistic meal. The dynamism of the Christian celebration is expressed by that procession and the general movement toward the East which it involves.

Let us add that, of course, in the Syrian churches which have remained faithful to their early tradition, there are no other seats but those of the clergy. Therefore the whole assembly, far from being a static mass of spectators, remains an organic gathering of worshippers, first centered on the ark, for hearing and meditating upon the scriptures, and finally going toward the East all together, for the eucharistic prayer and the final communion.

A last point must be underlined. The presence of the clergy among the faithful, in the primitive churches as in the synagogues, emphasizes the fact that, in spite of its role of leadership, the "action" remains a collective action in which all take part together. There is not a worship of the clergy performed for the passive attendance of the congregation, but a congregational worship in which all pray together in the meditation of the word communicated by the ministers, and participate with them in a common eucharist, by their offering, their responses to the consecration prayer and their communion. The presiding bishop or priest acts always as the center of the whole body assembled around him, either at the *bema* or at the altar. Never as a single performer before an audience having only to look at him. Also, if he is at the center of the gathering, he is always referring it, and himself, not to himself, but to a transcendent focus: the word of the Gospel, the table of the word made flesh and our food, and finally the eternal advent of the Lord of whom he is only the minister. Such a worship is certainly hierarchical, but in the sense of being an organic worship where every member has his own role to play at his own place, while nobody remains passive, the whole body acting together in unity.

To conclude we must answer a last question. Why is it that, of all the various combinations between the seat, the *bema* and the Ark, which had been tried freely in the synagogues, that only has been retained by the Syrian churches which groups together in the center of the building these three elements? The answer seems evident: to make possible a full participation of the women themselves while keeping them apart from the men. We must reckon this point as a last major difference between the Jewish and the Christian worship.

We must not for all that exaggerate the difference. Women were not excluded from the Jewish worship, either of the Temple or of the synagogue. In the Temple, they had a court reserved for them, behind that where the men alone were admitted, the men themselves having no admittance to the third and priestly court. In the ancient synagogues, we have no clear attestation of the place to which the women could have access. Their attendance was never required, but it is certain that it was not only accepted but encouraged. In later synagogues, they will have tribunes or boxes for their own use. It seems that, in the ancient synagogues as in the Temple, they were admitted to stand behind the men.

However, in Israel, the men alone were considered as having part in that common priesthood of all the holy people already described in Exodus XIX. On the men alone, therefore, rested the duty of fulfilling the ceremonial law. Reciprocally, there was no regular synagogal worship where ten adult men were not present, whether there were women with them or not, in any number. The women were reduced to a role of prayerful attendance.

In the domestic worship, it was not so. Although they could not recite the thanksgiving prayers, they took part in the religious meal. And some tasks were explicitly theirs, not only the preparation of the ritual food for the most sacred meals, as that of the Pasch, but also, for example, the lighting of the sabbath lights, and their introduction into the room, which was entrusted to the mother of the family.

But, from the beginnings of the Christian Church, the "kingly priesthood" of all the believers was extended in some measure to the women as well. They were still strictly required not to take to themselves the "ministry of the word" and its development into the ministry of the public prayer, especially of the eucharistic prayer. But they were to be baptized, exactly as the men, to receive the chrismal anointing, to take part in the collective prayers, to offer at the eucharist and to communicate. Therefore, room had to be provided for them, no only as for pious onlookers or hearers, but as for true partakers in the public worship.

In all the Syrian churches, and, it seems, in all or most of the churches of Christian antiquity, the church was therefore separated into two equal sections, and the *bema* was located between them. Thus, in the first part of the celebration, the bishop and other ministers had the women behind them and the men before. There were usually, because of that, two separate entrances on the side of the building, and, in the mediaeval buildings at least, maybe long before, a light barrier, north and south of the middle of the *bema,* delimited the respective places for men and women. However, it seems clear that the women as well as the men, at the offering and for communion, had to move to the altar.

III. THE ROMAN BASILICAS

Another type of Christian church arising from a somewhat different way of organizing the celebration was to appear later in Rome. On the origins of the specific Roman church many theories have been evolved, some of which are still lingering in many handbooks but most of which have been invalidated by recent archaeological research.[4]

The first one is that according to which the Roman church and its particular disposi-

[4] Cf. P. Testini, *Archeologia cristiana,* Rome, 1953; R. Vielliard *Recherches sur les origines de la Rome chretienne;* Rome, 1959 (2nd. ed.); N. Maurice-Denis Boulet, "La leçon des eglises de l'antiquite," *Maison-Dieu,* LXIII, (1960).

tion would have arisen from a primitive way of celebration: that of the catacombs. But the researches, especially of R. Vielliard, have made it perfectly clear that the so-called "church of the catacombs" is just a romantic fiction and has never existed. The idea that the Christian Church, in times of persecutions, could have developed a hidden life of worship in the catacombs is simply foolish. Not only the catacombs, that is the underground cemeteries of Rome, would have been at all times a most awkward place to hold a regular worship, but the idea of worshipping there would have immediately attracted the suspicion of the authorities. At times of persecutions the only place where the Roman Christians could have some relative security were the homes of friendly patricians. But it is now perfectly clear that long before the end of the persecutions the Christians, in Rome as elsewhere, had for their worship the regular use of buildings, either given to them or built especially for that purpose.

The later supposition, developed by Gregory Dix[5] among others, that the first Christian churches might have been, at least in

[5] See the first chapter of *The Shape of the Liturgy*, London, 1945.

Rome, ordinary houses of vast dimensions where the atrium, with the adjacent features already adapted to ritual pagan uses, could have served for worship, is no less fanciful. The atrium was a kind of cloister with a central part roofless, around an *impluvium,* a basin in which rain water was dripping from the roofs. No place could have been more inconvenient, either for the service of the word or for the eucharistic meal. The idea that the *impluvium* could have served for the baptismal fount and the *cartibulum* (the table for the old pagan home sacrifices) be used as a Christian altar is completely baseless and just ludicrous. Nothing of that can be based on any kind of archaeological or documentary evidence. The only place indeed, in a patrician house, which could have been used for Christian worship as for any kind of meeting, was the *triclinium,* that is to say a vast oblong dining hall, which, very often, took the shape of a basilica.

However, we know nothing actually of any triclinium which could ever have been used in that way, a fortiori nothing of the disposition it could have undergone for that purpose. Neither do we know anything of the disposition of the churches built in Rome before the end of the persecutions. The first evidence we have there concerns the first great Christian basilicas built with the imperial support under or after Constantine.

Moreover, most of these buildings themselves have come to us in a state resulting from later modifications, which do not seem to antedate Saint Gregory the Great (sixth century). In a few only, we can still detect something of what was their primitive organization, primitive here meaning such as it was when they were built after the conversion of Constantine (middle or second part of the fourth century). Such is still imperfectly the case of the Lateran basilica. Its reconstruction at the Renaissance has not altogether obscured or suppressed its primitive disposition. This is corroborated by many more churches in North Africa. Long before Christian times that province, of all the countries subjected to Rome, had been conspicuous for its close contacts with the imperial city and therefore for its most strict adherence to Roman uses. Still today, in Tunisia or Algeria, we have more possibilities of realizing what was a typical Roman city or house than anywhere in Italy, with the single exception of Pompei. In regard to churches, since North

African Christianity was practically extinguished by the Islamic conquest, what we find there may give us, similarly, a better view of the Constantinian churches, before later modifications, than anything still extant in Rome.[6]

In these churches, the most striking feature is that the seat of the bishop has been brought into the center of the apse and that it is now a throne: not just a teacher's *cathedra* but the seat of honor of a high dignitary. It is clear that this is only a reflection of the use of the basilica building for official purposes in ancient Rome. Even as the seat of the emperor himself in the Senate, the seat of the magistrate, especially in the basilica used as a judicial court, was of the same kind and had the same location. Around him, seated or standing according to their ranks, were his assessors or lower functionaries. It is agreed now by all the scholars that the installation, first of the bishop of Rome, in a similar situation, together with his clergy, is in its turn a reflection of the fact that, at the beginning of the Constantinian era, the bishop of Rome first

[6] Cf. F. van der Meer, *Augustine the Bishop: The Life and Work of a Father of the Church,* Engl. trans., New York, 1962.

or all and the other bishops together with him were officially assimilated to the high officers of the state. The concession (or assumption) of that quasi-imperial seat went together with the use of the candlesticks and the incense brought before them in procession, as they had been used long before to precede the imperial dignitaries. All that was the first beginnings of what is now commonly called "triumphalism," the origin of which lies in the fact that bishops had become authorities of the state.

The first and most obvious result of that is that the Christian leaders, now for the first time, tended to be regarded as authorities above and outside the Church, rather than an authority in the Church linked with her collective life. Hence the new separation, instead of a mere distinction, between clergy and faithful, completely unknown in the primitive Christian worship, as well as previously in the synagogue. The bishop having become a great lord, and being surrounded now with the ceremonial and insignia pertaining to his new status, the other ministries, instead of being, as they were primitively, the links of his solidarity with the whole people, tended for their part to become an impressive array of flunkeys, enhancing his own dignity while separating it from the *vulgum pecus*. Since the bishop sits now in imperial state in an exalted position, his clergy becomes his court itself, removed as far as possible from the rabble.

In spite of that basic modification, however, the primitive Constantinian basilica kept as much as possible of the more primitive disposition of the Christian churches, as we have found it in the early Syrian church. Since the bishop had taken to himself the primitive place of the altar, the altar was removed to where he himself had stood before: in the nave, more or less exactly in the centre of it (which must have meant generally between the men and the women). If the bishop and his ministers were not any longer in the midst of the people and the clergy for the first part of the liturgy, when the bishop finally went to the altar for the eucharistic meal, he had still all his people grouped around him, just as before, usually the men on one side, the women on the other.

The *bema* and the Ark themselves had not altogether disappeared but they had been modified. As we have explained it before, the Ark, at the times of the last persecutions, must have disappeared everywhere, at least from the Western churches. The *bema* itself could not any longer exist as a platform, which would have now made difficult the eucharistic procession from the episcopal throne to the altar. It was replaced by an oblong enclosure on the ground floor, opened at both ends, where the ministers of the lower ranks, readers or singers, stood together: the *schola.* One or two permanent ambos or pulpits, on both sides, were added to it for the readings. And if the first veil had disappeared with the Ark, the huge candlestick was kept, near the major ambo from which the Gospel would be read.

The altar itself, even though now in the midst of the people, had lost nothing of its dignity. Even as the throne of the bishop it was raised on steps, and a *ciborium,* a marble baldachino from which burning lamps were hanging, protected and enhanced its sacrality. Between the columns of the ciborium curtains were added, as an equivalent of the former veil. Milan even has kept something until now which might well have preceded the ciborium: what is called in the Ambrosian rite of today the *padigliano,* a big tent able to shelter the whole altar and open-

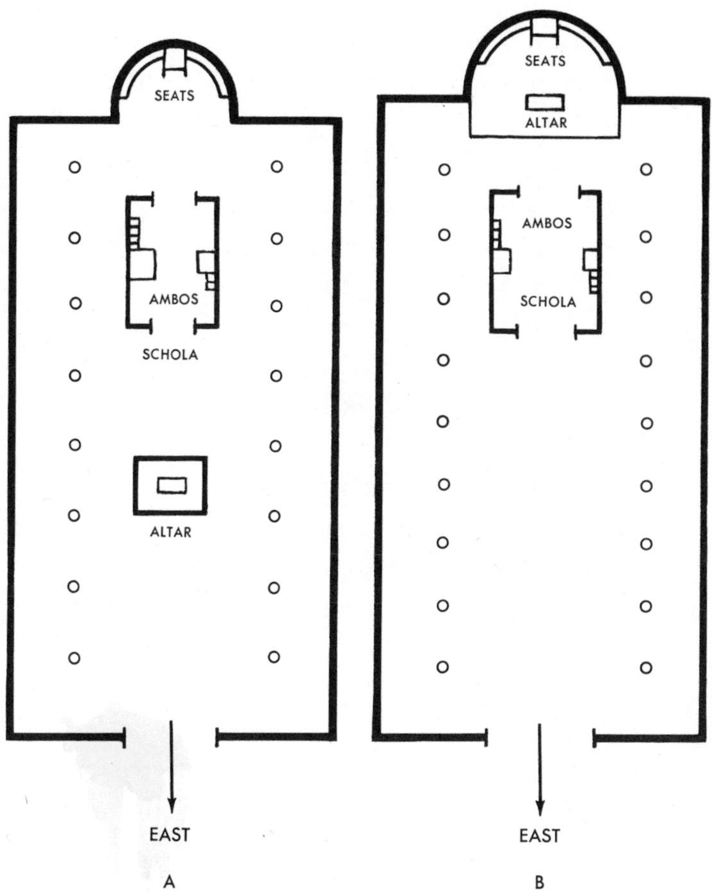

Fig. 3. Location of the altar in the Roman basilica-type church, in which *bema* and Ark were modified and later replaced by the *schola,* an oblong enclosure, open at both ends, where ministers, readers, and singers stood together.

ing for the entrance of either the officiants, the offerers or the communicants.

A later modification of that scheme was much more deeply to alter the whole character of the primitive celebration. Then not only would the bishop and the clergy be removed from the congregation for the first part of the service, but they would remain in their lofty isolation even for the eucharist. For the altar itself would have come to be moved to their own exclusive precinct. We know, from the life of Saint Gregory, that this last transformation was to be his work. Its immediate purpose was explicitly to bring the altar, in Saint Peter's, just above the tomb of the apostle. This has to be interpreted as a product of the growing desire to combine the eucharistic celebration with the cult of the martyrs. It had been customary, long before that, to have an anniversary celebration of the eucharist near their tombs. Later, for that occasion, the altar had been placed on the tomb itself. Soon it would be desired to have no celebration except on the tomb, or at least some relics, of a saint.

But we may suspect a secondary motive behind that modification of the disposition of the Roman basilicas. Formerly, all the worship in the church as all the worship in the synagogue had been a collective worship, of the whole body of the believers. Very soon, in the Constantinian period, with a sudden influx of converts of a very uncertain fervor, we can see the beginning of great changes. Saint Chrysostom already complains in his sermons that many people now attend the eucharistic celebration without communicating. Saint Augustine was not so pessimistic but it was already clear, from what he says, that there was in Africa also a tendency toward that. No longer was the communicant attendance taken for granted. In Rome itself it seems no less clear that, very early, only a spiritual elite among the laity was regularly attending the solemn papal station. In the middle ages the communion of the faithful would even disappear entirely from the papal mass. It would never be reintroduced as a normal practice until the last popes, John XXIII and Paul VI. In fact, one of the great achievements of Gregory the Great was to provide the Roman basilicas with monastic communities celebrating daily a more and more elaborate liturgy, but not so much for the Christian people as instead of them. We can see at that time the regular celebration becoming no longer a public collective celebration of the whole Church, but a semi-private celebration of a community of monks and clerics, inside a Church scarcely occupied by lay worshippers. The disappearance long before St. Gregory of the papal homily, and the semi-monastic character of his own homilies when he tried to restore the practice, is a telling witness of the fact.

In such circumstances, it is easily conceivable that the pope would have thought it absurd, in order to celebrate the eucharist with his monasticized clergy, to move from the presbytery in the apse to a far distant altar in the middle of a nearly empty nave. By removing the altar to the tomb of the apostle, he was not only magnifying the cult of his first predecessor but making possible a simplified and more rational celebration, since the altar would be now in direct contact with the basic and often more numerous part of the congregation: monks and clerics. This, of course, meant, after a previous injection of secular triumphalism, a clericalisation of the eucharist itself.

At that time, if not before, we must add that at Saint Peter's, the great apse of the presbytery was separated from the nave not only by a chancel, a slight barrier which had always existed in the secular use of the basilica, to separate the magistrate and his officers from the crowd. A double row of columns, now, enclosed the apse, making of it an *ecclesiola in ecclesia,* purely clerical. There is still discussion between the scholars to know whether Gregory brought the altar just before the columns or behind them. When the old Constantinian basilica was pulled down during the Renaissance, it is clear that the altar was *behind.* As we know of no other major modification of the church during the middle ages, it is probable that that was already the place where Gregory had brought it. The supposition seems to be supported by the fact that in the stational churches, where the new disposition of Saint Peter's was soon imitated, the altar has been usually removed behind a *pergula,* a lighter but not lower barrier than the columns of Saint Peter's.

Such is the way in which what we call now "the altar facing the people" came into existence.

In Rome itself, it does not seem that this disposition has ever become universal. First the Lateran cathedral, as we have said before, where the greatest celebrations of the year could be expected to gather a great crowd, kept to the older use, that of the altar at the centre of the nave. It is practically the only one which has been found as still extant in the African churches at the disappearance of African Christianity.

But the persistence of an even earlier use in Rome, similar to that of the early Syrian churches, is attested even long after Saint Gregory and even in a major basilica. The *Liber pontificalis* tells us that, two centuries after Saint Gregory, Pope Pascal I, at Saint Mary Major, had still his seat in the middle of the nave, with the men before him and the women behind, the altar being in the apse. What caused him then to move the pontifical throne to the apse, behind the altar, was, we are told, his displeasure at hearing the women, behind his back, commenting upon what he said to his deacons.

All these facts, and these are all the facts we have concerning the origin of the altar "facing the people," show that the disposition made famous by Saint Peter's of Rome, and most of the other basilicas in Rome which have followed its example, is undoubtedly of some great antiquity and authorized by the long practice of the popes. But they no less clearly show that it has come into being through a whole process which is not at all what many people fondly imagine today. What is more important is that its original significance had little or nothing to do with that which has been attributed to it in modern times.

First of all, far from being primitive, it is a late product (not anterior to the sixth century) of a rather complex evolution. All that which we know, either of the primitive celebration or of the celebration which arose in the Constantinian era, points to an altar either in the end of the building or in the middle of the nave. In the first case there were no people at all whom the celebrant could face. In the second case, the only people he faced were a part of the congregation, which seems to have been made exclusively of the women.

The idea that a celebration facing the people must have been the primitive one, and that especially of the last supper, has no other foundation than a mistaken view of what a meal could be in antiquity, Christian or not. In no meal of the early Christian era, did the president of the banqueting assembly ever face the other participants. They were all sitting, or reclining, on the convex side of a sigma table, or of a table having approximately the shape of a horse shoe. The other side was always left empty for the service. Nowhere in Christian antiquity, could have arisen the idea of having to "face the people" to preside at a meal. The communal character of a meal was emphasized just by the opposite disposition: the fact that all the participants were on the same side of the table.

The use of a round or square table for meals, with the eaters sitting all around, is a late medieval practice, coming probably from Germanic or Scandinavian countries. The "round table," of King Arthur and his knights could not have existed before that. And, even through the medieval period, the use for state banquets of a semi-circular table, with everybody sitting on the convex side, remained the common use.

To this it must be added that the description of the late Roman use as of an altar "facing the people" is purely modern. The phrase was never used in Christian antiquity and it is equally unknown in the middle ages. It makes a first appearance in the rubrics of the Roman missals printed in the XVIth century. Then, the priest, being ordered to turn "versus populum" to say "Dominus vobiscum," is cautioned that, if the disposition of the altar is such that he is in that situation already, at least concerning a notable part of the congregation, he need not turn.

Never, and nowhere, before that, have we any indication that any importance, or even attention, was given to whether the priest celebrated with the people before him or behind him. As Professor Cyrille Vogel has recently demonstrated it, the only thing ever insisted upon, or even mentioned, was that he should say the eucharistic prayer, as all the other prayers, facing East. In cases, not uncommon, it seems, when, with an altar either in the nave or at the chord of the apse, the East was not on the side opposite to the apse, but still, as primitively, on the side of the apse, the celebrant, going to the altar, was explicitly directed to turn around it. Similarly, in the first part of the service, when he had been praying at his throne, he had been praying turned toward the back of his seat, exactly as it is prescribed in the Mischnah for the rabbis and the elders, when they had the back of their seats in the direction of Jerusalem.

A last detail must be made clear in this connection. Even when the orientation of the church enabled the celebrant to pray turned toward the people, when at the altar, we must not forget that it was not the priest alone who, then, turned East: it was the whole congregation, together with him. Such a position, indeed, was never a priestly peculiarity. From a very early period, it had been requested of every Christian in prayer, and especially emphasized as his only normal position when attending the eucharistic prayer. At the beginning of this, in the Egyptian liturgy especially, the deacon always reminded the people: "Turn to the East!" That, therefore, in churches with what we now call an altar facing the people, must have had the awkward effect of having a part at least (sometimes the major part) of the assembly turning their backs to the altar during the whole of the consecration prayer. This may well explain why it is that such a way has always remained an almost purely Roman peculiarity, as we shall see it soon.

However, even when the people were in a position to see something of what was happening at the altar, there was very little to see. For, in the patristic era, once the offerings had been brought there and the eucharistic prayer had started, there was not any longer anything to see. The celebrant, then, was just praying with his hands extended, as everybody did at the time, without a single gesture either of himself or of his attendants, from beginning to end. Even if we suppose that, at this moment, the curtains of the ciborium were drawn open, it would have been perfectly useless to peep at what the pope or bishop might be doing. They were just praying, as anybody else in the whole church. The only difference between the celebrant and the others was that he was praying aloud, the others being supposed to follow what he said, in order to give their Amen at the end.

Today, of course, there are plenty of gestures of the celebrant during the canon, the discovery of which may amuse the laity for some time when, having been accustomed to the other way, they experience for the first times the so-called celebration facing the people: plenty of signs of the cross, of kissing the altar, handling and elevating the elements, and, especially after the consecration, numberless genuflexions (in this last case, however, what they see indeed is just the periodical disappearance of the celebrant). But nothing of that existed in the patristic period. The manipulation of the elements at the moment of the narrative of the institution has been introduced only in the middle ages. Later, the signs of the cross, which have been multiplied only at a very late period, then the elevations, were added, the second elevation being somewhat older (probably eighth century) than that which has followed the consecration since the thirteenth century. All the genuflexions are nearly post-medieval.

As Professor Cyrille Vogel has made perfectly clear, the most important point behind all that is that we must not confuse participating in the celebration with looking at it. The practice of looking curiously at the eucharistic elements themselves, especially at the time of the consecration, is a practice completely unknown to Christian antiquity. It was introduced only in the late thirteenth century, together with the double elevation at that moment. More generally, the concentration on seeing what the officiants do, far from having ever accompanied a real participation of all in the liturgy, has appeared as a compensation for the lack of this participation, and is psychologically more or less exclusive of it. In the Orthodox churches, in which, of all contemporary churches, the feeling of the whole community of the worshippers that they take part in the whole celebration is at its maximum, the desire as well as the possibility of seeing what the priest is doing is at its minimum. It is perfectly understandable: either you look at somebody doing something for you, instead of you, or you do it with him. You can't do both at the same time. In Christian antiquity, even if the bishop or priest alone said the eucharistic prayer, all the Christians, clergy and laity, praying with him, in the same position, in the same direction, answering him at the preface and at the conclusion, were perfectly aware of the fact that what he said was said in the name of all. The idea of him turning to them, or them turning to him, so that they could see him doing the eucharist, could not arise, and, in fact, never arose, except long after they had completely ceased to think that he did it, not just for them, but with them.

It may indeed be wondered whether one of the first factors, in Rome itself, which led to the quite medieval idea that the clergy celebrated the liturgy for the faithful, and even instead of them, but not with them, was not the removal of the clergy in an apse outside the community. This idea must have become irresistible when the altar itself was brought to this new and purely clerical sanctuary, so that the whole liturgy now took place, from the point of view of the faithful, behind the altar. To look at it from afar was now all that they could do. The celebration had now ceased altogether to be theirs. The altar facing the people, historically, therefore, far from having been ever intended for a common celebration, seems to have been both the effect and a cause of a substitution of a clerical celebration for a corporate worship.

IV. THE BYZANTINE CHURCHES

The traditional Byzantine church is another departure from the primitive church, the elaboration of which must have been approximately contemporaneous with that of the Roman basilica. But while this last one is characterized first of all by a strong influence of the pre-Christian and secular use of the basilica which modified its early Christian use, the first one was a logical outgrowth of this Christian use out of the basilica itself. The Byzantine architects discarded all the features of the pre-Christian basilica which were not adapted to the Christian liturgy, so that they evolved a new type of building where everything was there only for its own purpose. The Byzantine church, certainly, proceeded from the old Syrian church, but it dropped all its features, anterior to its liturgical adaptation of the basilica either by the Jews or the Christians, which had nothing to do with either Jewish or Christian worship, remodelling the others with this, and nothing but this, in view.[7]

For it must be admitted that there were plenty of details in the hellenistic basilica which made it only, in the best possible circumstances, a second best to celebrate the Christian eucharist. First of all, the two rows of columns divided the inner space in such a way that only the central nave could house a united congregation, the aisles being left only to deambulation, or breaking the body of the worshippers in three distinct bodies, two of which could enjoy only a very limited participation. This was reinforced in the greater basilicas, where a double transept was added, between the apse and the main fabric of the building. If the lateral transepts were to be used, you had not only three but five different separate congregations, in addition to the clergy in the apse,

[7] Cf. Gervase Mathew, *Byzantine Aesthetics,* London, 1963.

trying to worship together. And even when the central nave alone was used, in big churches its length rendered very problematic the participation of the Western part of the congregation in the service of prayers and readings, and tended to nullify it altogether in the eucharistic celebration, whatever might be the situation of the altar. It was certainly for this that the women, allowed only then to a minor participation, were generally confined to this humiliated area.

All these major inconveniences were suppressed at a stroke by substituting for the oblong basilica, divided in three or more sections, a square building, with no columns at all. In the center of that building, under a circular cupola, the *bema,* with the ark, the lectern (or lecterns), the bishop's seat and the other seats for the priests could be easily installed, and even made more spacious, without constituting any hindrance for the people standing all around.

Then, for the small apse at the end, could also be substituted a much wider one, in which the altar would become both more prominent and more accessible for the whole congregation. A semi-cupola above it would enhance its importance much more easily than any ciborium, while contributing to the equilibrium of the whole structure, in combination with three other semi-cupolas on the three other sides. The western one would cover the narthex, for the catechumens and the penitents, while the northern and southern ones could house the choir. Thus, the whole congregation would be inserted into the choir itself, and much more easily taken into its singing, rather than tending to be excluded from a body of specialists performing in isolation.

Easily grouped around the bishop and the readers for the service of the word and the prayers, the assembly would after that open for the procession of the holy gifts and rearrange itself in such a way that it may be gathered around the altar, nothing separating it from the sacred meal.

Haghia Sophia of Constantinople, built, and rebuilt and completed after an earthquake, under Justinian would become the grandiose model of that new type of a Christian church, which may be the best adaptation to its purpose ever achieved in the past.

Later, in the mediaeval period, the process of clericalisation and monasticization of the Christian worship would appear in Constanti-

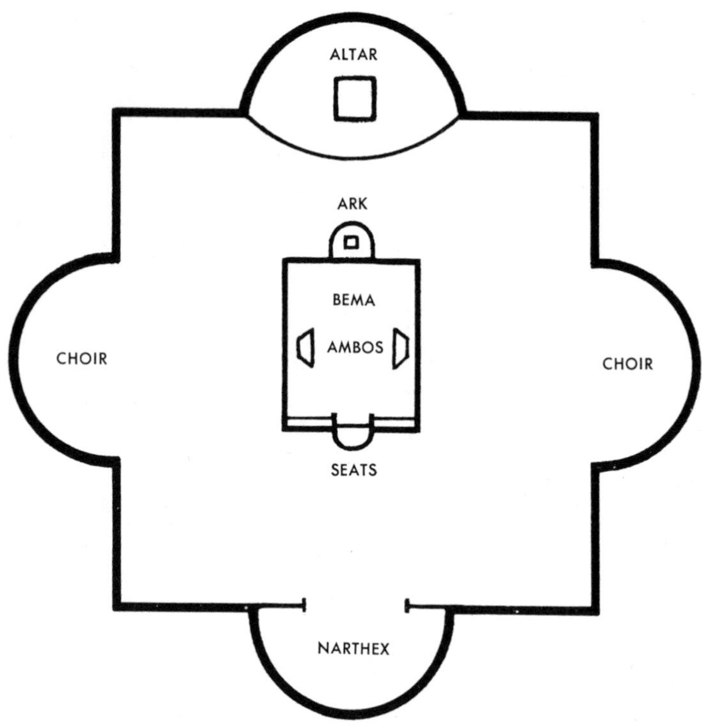

Fig. 4. Location of the altar in the early Byzantine church, ideally arranged for the assembly grouped around the bishop and readers to proceed with the offertory and later gather around the altar. Today there is a single lectern (rather than ambo) in the center of the *bema* (facing the altar). This may have existed even before the Ark disappeared.

nople and all the East as well as in Rome and the West. But, in such a building, it would never have the effect of creating a clerical or monastic church inside the church of everybody. When the stalls of the numerous monks and clergy will make their appearance, they will be located all around the church, the stall of the bishop being the first at the right of the entrance, and that of the monastic superior at the left, the two halves of the choir remaining on both sides. For the penitential office of Matins, another monastic choir will be arranged, in the same way, around the narthex. Therefore, even when the monks and clerics will celebrate almost alone, they will never be separated from a possible congregation, but rather always ready to welcome it in their midst.[8]

Sooner or later, in imitation of the Constantian basilicas of the first imperial city, a throne in the apse, surrounded by a bench for the priests, will be introduced. But the central *bema* will never disappear for that. Only the reading of the Gospel will be transferred to the *solea,* a secondary *bema* at the entrance

[8] See the description of Haghia Sophia in Germanus, *Historia ecclesiastica* and in the poem on the subject by Paul the Silentiary.

of the sanctuary. The other liturgical readings will continue to be made from the earlier and central one. And, at least for the pontifical liturgy, this will remain the usual place of the main celebrant for the first part of the celebration.

A very important feature of the Byzantine church will be the development of the iconography, which will tend, in its earlier phase especially, to emphasize the collective, and even the cosmic, character of the celebration. Far from concentrating exclusively the sacredness of the place on the altar and the clerical sanctuary immediately connected with it, it will underline the introduction of the whole body of the worshippers into the Christian mystery, and, with them, of the whole world.

The first origins of the Christian iconography, and more especially of the iconography connected with the liturgy, have been sought in many quarters, through all kinds of more or less ingenuous conjectures. But now these origins have become perfectly clear. For this, as so many other elements in the primitive Christian worship, proceeds from the synagogal worship. Sukenik, who has studied most of all the ancient synagogues from which something has come down to us, has made it clear beyond all doubt that the opposition of the Jews to any kind of iconographical decoration of the synagogues is not at all primitive. It has developed only as an anti-Christian reaction, and not before the late third or early fourth century of our era. The older synagogues were abundantly decorated with representations of selected biblical episodes. These were clearly understood as being not just memories of the past but an embodiment of a notion underlying the whole Haggadah or traditional interpretation of the Jewish worship. According to it, the Jewish festivals were a permanent participation of the People in the high deeds of God for them in the past. The earliest Christian representations, found not only in the catacombs but also in some of the earlier church buildings, follow closely the older Jewish selection of these facts and apply to them a renewed Christian interpretation. But, however new, this interpretation is in line with the Jewish one. The meal of the Angels with Abraham or the sacrifice of Isaac are not any longer images of the covenant perpetually re-enacted through the sacrifices of the Temple, but now of the eucharist. Noah in the ark, similarly, is not just a reminder of the Exodus and the salvation through the Red Sea, but of baptism. And so on. But both the selection of the biblical themes and their treatment are so clearly in continuity that some archaeologists are still reluctant to admit that the synagogue of Doura Europos, for an example, was really a synagogue, and not a judaeo-christian church, since its decoration is so strikingly similar to that of a contemporary church, equally found there. But, as Sukenik has established it, the only difference between the synagogue of Doura Europos and the other contemporary synagogues is that special circumstances, at Doura Europos, have led to an uncommon preservation of an ensemble of frescoes, the equivalent of which are witnessed everywhere, but only through a few scattered fragments.

In the Byzantine church, the Christian iconography, for the first time, will find the possibility of a full and coordinated development.

The central cupola will be occupied by some frescoe or mosaics depicting the *Christos pantokrator,* the risen Christ established in His glory, with the book of the Gospels in His right hand. He dominates the whole creation, visible and invisible, with both the Angels and the saints on the pendentives of the cupola and the earthly congregation below making a single gathering. In the cupola of the apse, the Blessed Virgin is seen ascending toward her Son, as the *Ecclesia orans,* interceding for the whole world, together with the apostles. Immediately above the altar, on two related registers, the last supper will be visible, dominated by the heavenly liturgy of the Angels bearing through the heavens the instruments of the passion.

Later, on the *pergula* supporting the curtains or veils before the altar, other, formerly portative, icons will make their appearance, connecting with both Jesus and Mary on earth the Angel of the Annunciation and the Baptist, together with the patron saints of the local community. But long before that, on the lower part of the walls, processions of martyrs and virgins had appeared already, bringing their offerings to the heavenly altar, just as the worshippers were to bring theirs to the earthly one, the two being mystically identified.

All this was only a projection in painting or in mosaics of the vision of the Church assembled together for worship, as it had been developed especially by the *Mystagogy* of Maximos the Confessor, or the *Historia ecclesiastica* (which means here "the description of the church") ascribed to Germanus of Constantinople. It is not to be wondered, after that, if the Russian ambassadors sent to Constantinople to bring back its Christianity to their country could describe the Christian eucharist in the Temple of the Holy Wisdom by saying: "We have seen the heavens on the earth." Legendary or not, the saying expresses a fact: the most successful attempt, maybe, in the whole history of the Christian church, to make the invisible visible in Christian worship.

V. THE WESTERN CHURCHES

The most common types of Western churches appear to be other developments of the primitive Christian church, as we find it in the early Syrian basilicas. These are different from the Byzantine development insofar as they never completely outgrew and discarded the structure of the basilica itself. On the other hand, the typical Roman modification of its use for Christian worship does not seem to have been ever influential in the West, outside of Rome itself, except in a few places in Italy and in Northern Africa. The most common disposition, especially in France, England and Germany, which has come to us through the middle ages, simply betrays the progressive clericalisation of worship by the fact that the *bema,* together with the seats of the bishop and clergy, has been brought most of the times into the immediate vicinity of the altar. At a date which cannot be ascertained exactly, probably already in the early middle ages, that chancel or choir, as it came to be called, was fenced from the main part of the church by a screen. The screen itself, at least in collegiate churches, came to be a wall, with only a central door leaving a scanty vision of what was happening inside but barring almost completely the people in the nave from any possiblity of participation.[9]

In fact, the offertory procession having disappeared, the communion of the faithful become exceptional, most of the singing performed by the choir, and the whole service of the word itself unintelligible, from the use of a now dead language, understood only by the clerics, there was nothing in which they

[9] Cf. especially the first chapter of G. W. O. Addleshaw and F. Etchells, *The Architectural Setting of Anglican Worship,* London, 1948, for what follows.

could have taken part any longer. When they were present, the most pious among the laity were taught to pursue their own devotions, more or less parallel with the liturgy but unconnected with it, by saying their beads or, the few more learned among them, reading some book of private meditation.

After the thirteenth century, the elevation of the host concentrated their eucharistic devotion on the adoration of the presence at the time of the consecration. This may be considered as the beginning of the modern tendency to substitute for actual participation a mere visualization. The ritual already was explained as a dramatic re-enactment of the life and passion of Christ. New ceremonies were incessantly introduced to support that most artificial conception which was soon to lead, in protestantism, to the total disintegration of all sacramental notions. At the Epiphany, the Magi could be seen bringing their gifts to the altar, or, on Easter Sunday, the disciples and holy women hastening to the empty tomb, while doves would come down from the ceiling on Whitsunday, at the singing of the *Veni, Sancte Spiritus.*

Some more or less redeeming features, nevertheless, should not be forgotten. First

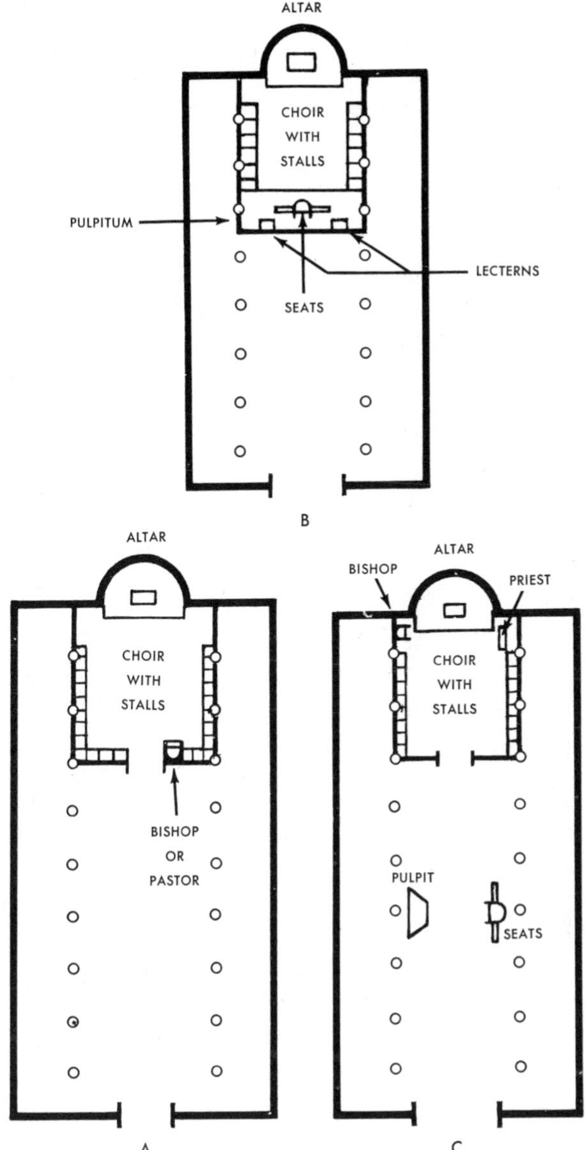

Fig. 5. Eastern arrangement in Western churches, showing progressive clericalization of worship. The people in the nave were almost completely barred from any possibility of participation.

of all, the development of the screen into a solid wall had its counterpart in many churches. On that wall, at the entrance of the chancel, a bridge was erected, called jube or pulpitum. On it, the readers made their appearance in view of the whole congregation, to sing to them the epistle and Gospel. From the jube also, the homily could be addressed to them. And although, usually, the seat of the bishop, or of the pastor in a parish, was now inside the screen, immediately at the right hand of the central door, it seems that this also, at least for solemn public celebrations, could be raised on the pulpitum. We know, for an example, that it was always the case in the cathedral church of Reims when the French kings were coronated.[10]

It must be added that the pulpitum, as a central place in the first part of the celebration, was always decorated, as the altar itself, by a great crucifix (the "rood") between candlesticks with burning tapers. It had, in fact, become an interesting equivalent of the primitive *bema.*

Beginning with the twelfth century, one must also reckon with an effort to reintro-

[10] Cf. the old work of J. B. Thiers, *Dissertation ecclésiastiques . . .*, Paris, 1688.

duce, between the first part of the mass, when the service of readings and prayers had become almost completely clericalised, and the offering of the eucharist, a reduplication in the vernacular of that first part. This is what has been called the prone in the French churches. It was soon very popular as well in Germany and in England. It has not yet attracted the attention of the scholars as much as it is worth. Its origin seems to be found in the renewal of popular instruction which went together with the foundation of the mendicant orders, especially the franciscans and dominicans. It was to produce another equivalent of the old *bema,* namely the pulpit, erected in the centre of the nave, usually on the North side (the Gospel side in these churches). Together with the pulpit, a secondary seat for the bishop or celebrant and the clergy was to appear on the other side, just in front of it (what, in French churches, is still called the "banc d'oeuvre").

From the pulpit, not only preaching was to be had, but a whole service to be conducted. It included, after a second reading in the vernacular, at least of the Gospel, but sometimes also of the other scriptural lessons, sometimes a catechism, with questions and answers to be rehearsed between the minister and the congregation, and some vernacular equivalent of the ancient "oratio fidelium" after the sermon. The traditional English "bidding prayer" finds there its origin. In Germany, but also in Italy, hymns in the vernacular could be added.

The Counter-Reformation, in most places, not only kept but greatly contributed to institutionalize and develop the prone. It also tended toward the suppression of the screen, which disappeared altogether in the churches newly erected at that time. Thus the people could fully see and follow the eucharistic celebration itself, if not yet regain their participation in it. Unfortunately this had its counterpart in the disappearance of the pulpitum, which led to the generalized and most unfortunate practice of reading the epistle and Gospel in the altar sanctuary itself, even at a high mass, when it was not, in the case of a mass said or sung by a single priest, at the altar itself.

In the countries of the ambrosian rite only, Milan and Northern Italy, the lessons of scripture have always been read, up to our times, by the reader, subdeacon and deacon, from the pulpit, as a full substitute for the ancient *bema*.

At the end of the middle ages also and at the Renaissance, the altar came to be dominated by a reredo: a more or less elaborated combination of paintings and sculptures. Too often the reredo was developed for itself, so as to reduce the altar to a pretext. But, even in the Baroque period, reredos expressing a theme closely connected with the eucharist, and emphasizing the foretaste of eternal glory to be found in the eucharistic celebration, are to be found, much more often than it is generally supposed. When treated in such a way, the reredo may have been a not unworthy equivalent of the deeply theological and liturgical decoration of the East wall and cupola in the Byzantine churches of the best period. It must not be forgotten that the recent rediscovery of Romanesque and Othonian wall paintings has shown the great influence that this Eastern tradition has had in the West for a long time. The frescoes of Saint-Savin-sur Gartempe, or of Berzé-la-ville, to mention only two examples, are witnesses of much more community between the iconographical tradition of East and West than it is commonly supposed. A composition like the *Mys-*

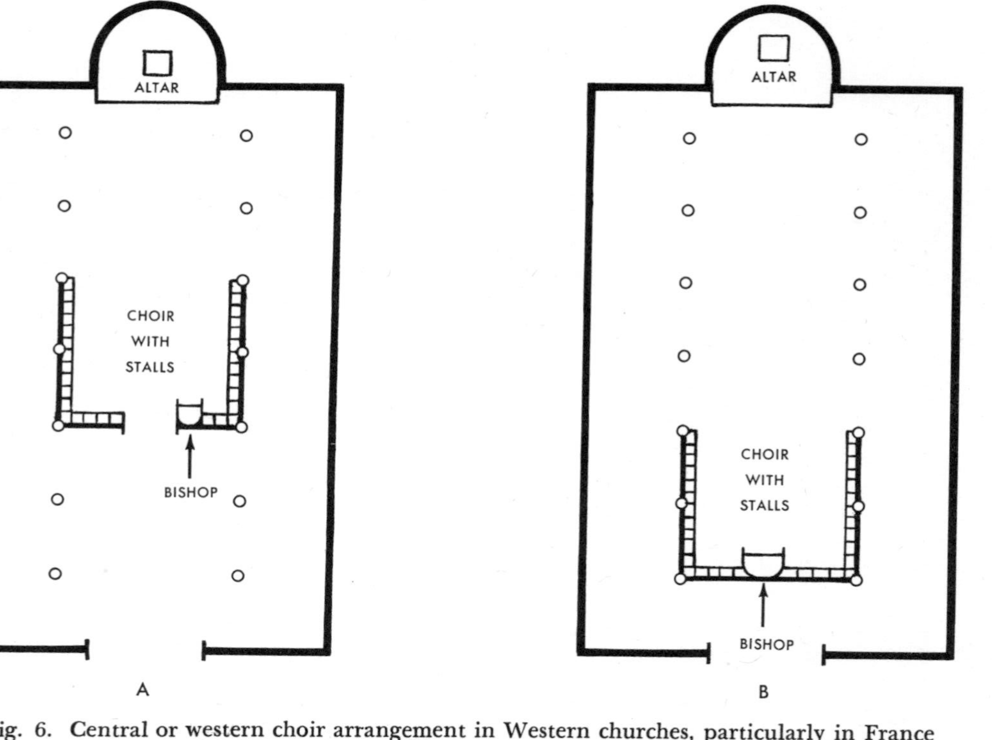

Fig. 6. Central or western choir arrangement in Western churches, particularly in France and England, where at least a sizable number of the congregation had access to participation. In German churches the western choir is generally in a second apse.

tical Lamb of Ian van Eyk is enough to assure us that the tradition could still be revived at the end of the middle ages, to be prolonged even into the best of the Baroque, especially in its more popular forms, in Southern Germany or French Brittany.

Another thing which we must remember is that the disposition of the chancel barring the people from any access to the altar, however prevalent, was never universal in the middle ages. In Spain especially, very often, the developed and enclosed choir was never moved from its primitive place in the centre of the nave. Such was also the case of French or English churches, like Saint-Benoit-sur-Loire or Westminster abbey. There, an important part at least of the congregation, either in the Eastern part of the nave or in the two transepts, could still follow the whole development of the liturgy, even if it was only as spectators.

In other, maybe more numerous, churches, in Spain or also in Germany, the clerical choir was moved not to the East but the West. There, the faithful, far from being rejected outside the celebration, were, at least materially, always included in it.

Even in churches where the chancel and the

altar sanctuary were enclosed into an inner church separated from the church of the faithful, at least from the twelfth century onward, one other, or more generally two other, altars were often introduced in the nave. It is true that they were not used generally for the public celebration but for more or less private masses. Nevertheless, they maintained some possibility, for the more devout of the people, of a more immediate access to the eucharistic celebration.

We must also remember that, in the Western churches, until the seventeenth century at least (in Italy even much later than that), there were still no seats for the congregation, except for a few dignitaries. In the large choirs of the cathedral or collegiate churches, on the other hand, there was much room left between the stalls of the clerics and choristers, which may well have been used by the male part of the lay attendance. This seems to have been not only tolerated but positively encouraged by the clergy, at least since the XVIIth century, and maybe long before that. The common use, still universal in the rural parishes of Western France, of having the men and the children seated in the choir itself.

the women only remaining in the nave, is a lasting witness of such a practice.

These details make it manifest that the tradition of worship, in the Western churches, all through the medieval period and up to the beginning of the modern era, was far more supple than we might be tempted to believe it now. It is only the XIXth and XXth centuries which, first by introducing unmovable pews for the faithful in the nave, then by reducing to preaching only the use of the pulpit, while suppressing the "banc d'oeuvre" and all that could remain of the old pulpitum or jube, have made of our churches just the equivalent of showrooms or classrooms, where a passive congregation has only to see from afar a clerical performance and passively to hear a clerical instruction.

In opposition to this recent impoverishment, and in spite of obvious defects (the result of a clericalisation of the liturgy which was more marked in the West than anywhere else), with the use of the pulpitum, as in case of an Eastern choir, and even without that, as in case of a central or Western choir, our medieval churches could easily have been used until their final deterioration for a worship as fully genuine and lively as that of the primitive Church. With the appearance of the later pulpit and "banc d'oeuvre" they could have proved almost as satisfactory as the primitive Byzantine churches. In fact, when the great liturgical renaissance of the seventeenth and eighteenth centuries was at its height in France and Germany, they certainly housed one of the best types of Christian worship ever achieved in the West.

The only thing the mediaeval and modern West always ignored, until quite recently, was the typically Roman use of the Constantianian basilicas, with what we have come to call "the altar facing the people."

The supposition now widely entertained that such a disposition could or should have been practically universal until a later period in the middle ages, is deprived of any historical justification. We have indeed, north of the Alps, about 150 altars still extant in their original situation which may be securely dated as pertaining to the first millennium of the Christian era. The German archaeologist Braun having carefully studied all of them has come to the indisputable conclusion that, except for one or two, all of them could never have been used for a celebration "versus ad populum."[11] And not only in the liturgical documents have we no trace of a supposed change from this position to that which has always been universal [in West and East outside of Rome and Africa], but we have neither any trace of a change to it in conjunction with the progressive acceptance of the Roman rite in the empire of Charlemagne and later in Spain. Everywhere, when the Roman rite was taken over, the church, and most of the ceremonial, remained as before. All that was ever taken from the Roman rite in the mediaeval West was the text of some of the prayers and in a smaller measure the choice of the readings. It is rather Rome itself which has come gradually to accept most of the ceremonial ways of the other Western churches, much more than it has ever influenced them on this point.

The only attempt to influence in some way the Western practice, especially concerning the disposition of the churches, from the part of Rome, is to be found in the description of the ceremonies in a cathedral that in the seventeenth century the ceremonial of Patrizzi propagated everywhere in the Latin Church.

[11] Cf. J. Braun, *Der christliche Altar,* Munich, 1932 (2nd. ed.)

It did not dare to impose the disposition of the Roman basilicas but suggested, as an equivalent adapted to the classical disposition of the Western churches, the location of the bishop's throne near the sanctuary of the altar on the north side, and when the bishop is not the celebrant the use of a *scamnum,* a bench for the officiating priest, at the same level but on the other side. Even that very modest suggestion seems to have remained quietly ignored in many and maybe in most places until the ultramontane campaign of Dom Gueranger late in the nineteenth century.

We shall conclude our description of the Western church in the mediaeval and Renaissance period by two observations. One is the way in which the reserved sacrament was kept, and the other the survival of the Ark for scripture.

Nowhere the practice of keeping the sacrament in the church is ancient. In the primitive Church it was kept not only by the clergy but by the lay people in their own houses. Later, from what we can infer from the oldest *Ordines romani,* the *capsa* in which the sacred species were kept, as well as the books of scripture, were taken from the *sacrarium* (the sacristy) only for the eucharistic celebration.

But in many mediaeval churches we find at a rather early date the use of armaries or aumbries, in the North and South walls of the sanctuary, to keep both. All through the mediaeval times, in Normandy for an example, there were generally two aumbries in the North wall under the custody of the deacon, and one in the South wall under that of the subdeacon. In the Northern aumbries the sacrament and the book of the Gospel respectively were locked and other books for the lessons being put in the southern aumbry.[12]

The use, which persisted locally very late, of a hanging pyxid for the sacrament above the altar seems to be of equal antiquity. But in many places the insecurity of the practice made it used only at the time of the celebration, when the sacrament was taken from the aumbry to be removed to the pyxid.

In the thirteenth century the richly ornamented towers, usually on the north side of the altar, make their appearance to house the sacramental bread. It is only at the time of the Renaissance that they were both reduced in height and generally moved to a central place on the altar itself. However, in the

[12] Cf. A. King, *Eucharistic Reservation,* London, 1965.

cathedral and other collegiate churches especially, until quite recently, the so-called tabernacle will never be made a part of the high altar. A special chapel (usually the Lady chapel or another more or less spacious secondary chapel), will be considered as a better location than the usual place of the public celebration.

VI. TRADITION AND RENEWAL

Such are the main data of tradition concerning the disposition of the Christian temple in the Catholic and Orthodox Churches of East and West. It is clear that they offer many more possibilities than is commonly supposed. If we cease to assume that the average late nineteenth century church has set the rule for ever, we can discover in Christian history an astonishing variety of consecrated practice. It can afford the modern congregations and the architects working for them both a very wide freedom and an inexhaustible wealth of inspiration. It is the more so when we realize that never any one of these dispositions has appeared as canonical in itself and for itself. They were accepted only insofar as they made possible a celebration as fully expressible as it could be in given circumstances of its inner meaning and spontaneous dynamism. However varied the legacy of the past, therefore, we are not even limited by it. If we only realize the pattern of worship which these different forms all tried to embody, we are today as free as were the great Byzantine architects to invent new forms for our own times, as long as they will prove as well adapted to their purpose as those of the past. And nothing can forbid us to hope with the help of new techniques to be able even to find better ones.

The main interest of our historical survey must be to make us aware not so much of the already actualised possibilities of Christian worship as of the pattern of cultic action which underlies all the monuments of the past. The Christian worship, as it has been emphasized by the Conciliar Constitution on the liturgy, is the most powerful teaching of what Christianity is. This is certainly in continuity with the worship of the synagogue. However, this aspect of teaching must be rightly understood. Even in the synagogue where it could appear much more exclusive than in the Christian Church, the teaching which is at the core of the worship of the people of God was clearly a very special kind of teaching. It was the teaching of the word of God. Being the word of the living God, it is a word of life. The "knowledge of God" it was to create, therefore, was not an abstract knowledge. It was joyful obedience, conformity not only to the divine will but to the divine Name: to the personal life of God adopting us as His own. Therefore, finally, it was communion with the most holy presence of the living God among us.

That, in the synagogal worship, was emphasized by the fact that, looking at the ark of scripture, the Jews were at the same time looking at the Temple, at the dwelling place on earth of the divine Shekinah. There it had been the center of worship, a worship which even then meant a whole life assuming a liturgical character of obedient service in thanksgiving.

The same thing in the Christian church is made even more actual from the fact that, reading the word of God and praying in response to that word, we are moved toward the altar, the table of the eucharistic banquet. The holy table in its turn points beyond itself to the symbolic East, the eschatological image of the *parousia* of the heavenly Jerusalem, where the people of God will be congregated for ever in the "panegyry," the eternal feast of the elect, in the immediate presence of God, glorified in the whole Body of the risen Christ.

A second point clearly connected with this is that this worship, inaugurated here and now to be achieved fully in the eternal kingdom, is the worship of a priestly people. This means what the Conciliar Constitution again emphasizes: that the celebration must develop an intelligent, active and fruitful participation of all the faithful together. Certainly this is not to be opposed to some special function (liturgies, in the meaning of a public sacred service, as Saint Clement says). The bishop or celebrating priest has to preside at the gathering in the Name of Christ Himself, and therefore to preach the apostolic word with authority, to apply it to the needs of the local congregation, and finally to consecrate the communal meal through the great eucharistic prayer. The deacon and ministers of the lower orders are to help him in that task, in such a way that all may participate as fully as possible by prayer in response to the word, a common offering, and finally a common participation in the sacrificial-sacramental meal.

The ministers, in such a view, are not acting for the people in the sense of acting instead of them, as from above and outside the community, upon sacred realities the others would have only to receive passively through hearing, seeing, or even being provided with a ready-made supernatural gift for which they would have no responsibility. The people have to receive that which they have offered, even if it is true that it has been transformed into a higher reality through the process of the common worship. What they have to receive in the communion, as Saint Augustine says, is the mystery of themselves, their own being accepted by Christ and inserted as it were into His own being, their own life hav ing become a part of His own life.

Therefore the ministers are normally not to be separated from the community but to be active in the midst of it, and in such a way as to associate it as fully as possible to what they do individually for it as a whole. The individual prayer, offering, communion are an integral part, on the other hand, of the public worship. It is not just some consequence of a clerical worship existing in itself and for itself. It is, we can say, the material itself on which the ministers are to work to consecrate it, and they cannot do that without the constant association with them of the whole people of which they are the leaders.

This means that to the three focuses of the celebration: the communication of the word, the altar around which all are to be gathered as the effect of their response to the word, the parousia toward which they are finally to be oriented, the clergy, not even the celebrant, are not to be added as a fourth focus. From the beginning unto the consummation, they are to be among the congregation and with it, as a ferment or leaven in the mass, to unite it progressively first through the word and the common prayer, then through the common offering and the common sacrificial meal, in view of the final consummation when God in Christ will be all in all.

In the first part of the celebration, therefore, the clergy are to gather around themselves the faithful by the meditation of the word, helping them to receive the word in the fully active response of a common faith expressed in a common prayer.

In the second part, they are, on the basis of that common response of faith, to lead them toward the holy table where they are all in Christ to be both offerers and partakers. Having received in time the realities of the eternal world under the sacramental veil, the people of God are to be sent back to this world of here and now, but in such a way and with such a presence in themselves that they may go through it together toward the final encounter with Christ. They will do that by consecrating to Him in their daily life everything in this transitory world in view of the eternal kingdom.

Such is the pattern of the Christian worship and such its dynamism that the actual celebration is to make as effective as possible through its visible manifestations. Therefore, everything in our churches has to be fully harmonized with that pattern and made fully subservient to its development.

When this has been understood the first thing which must be evident is that the temple, which is to house the church congregated into one, with the living Christ in the midst of her, should tend to create such a conjunction, or at least have nothing which can be a hindrance to its achievement. Whenever it is possible all those relics of the basilica which tend to divide the congregation into separate blocks—those who are in the nave and those who are relegated to the aisles, and where there is a transept those members who are in both parts of the transept—should be discarded by architects, as they were discarded by the first Byzantine builders.

From the point of view of the gathering, it could be supposed at first sight that the ideal building for the Christian Church would be a circular temple with altar, pulpit or ambo and seat of the celebrant near the centre. In fact, this has never been done and it is easy to understand that it is not just a matter of chance. A circular building with the people gathered around a central single focus would tend to create a community closed upon itself and would favor a static conception of worship. In opposition to both points, it is essential to the local gathering of the Christian Church first to remain open: open to the invisible gathering not only of the saints in heaven, but also of all the other Christian communities; open to the world itself in which the people of God have to perform the ministry of the kingly priesthood. No less essential is it to the celebration to be a development, a progress, our common engagement into the process of reaching the heavenly city. We are not gathered in the church to remain there but to start into a common pilgrimage in and through the world of here and now toward the eternal kingdom, the eschatological presence of the living God. Therefore the Christian church as the synagogue before it should be oriented along a common axis, so that the celebration may embody the progress from one focus to another, first the call of the word of God, then the ascension to the altar, and beyond the visible altar itself our further journey through this world to the next.

Here we meet the problem posed by the orientation of the church. In spite of the antiquity and the universality for many centuries of this use, is it to be maintained? Some will say that especially in modern cities it is not practical. The church must adapt itself to the local necessities in spite of respectable symbolisms. Others will go further and say that the orientation implied a kind of symbolism which is no longer significant to the modern man.

Whatever we may think of both objections, two points must be made clear. The first is that we must see not so much the materiality of the antique tradition as its meaning. If the material symbol itself cannot be kept, we must find some other way of expressing what it means. The fact that the eucharistic celebration has an eschatological orientation, that it is not a final step but that it looks toward a further consummation, needs certainly be emphasized in some way where the Christians gather for the eucharist.

The second point is that some kind of cosmic symbolism must be always present around the sacramental celebration. The sacramental world indeed must never become a world apart from the real world. It must give to it all a new meaning, impress upon it a new orientation. It is the whole world which has to regain from our sacramental experience a transparency to spiritual realities, and our renewed life in it has to tend to reorganize it toward these realities. Even if this cannot be achieved through the simple way of the traditional practice of praying facing East, it has to be done in some other way. An organization of the building, therefore, which leads toward the altar but does not stop at it, which points beyond it at some cosmic and supracosmic perspective, is greatly to be desired. Both the shape of the building and its decoration, as was the case in the churches of the past, will have to provide for the altar that double setting, in the world but not of this world, leading to another to which this has to be consecrated. Here the highest capacities of a living liturgical art combining the architectural design with a liturgical iconography are to find full play.

No less important is the plasticity the gathering of the people in the church is to preserve, in order to be able to follow in some way the orientation suggested, to develop the dynamism inherent in the liturgical assembly.

Here we come again to the problem created by the modern pews and more generally any kind of seats. The Eastern Christians have kept to the use common to them and to the West at least until the seventeenth century of standing most of the time, kneeling on the ground for short periods, but never sitting, exception being made, also for short periods, in favor of the priests and infirm or aged people. In the view of the modern Western Christian this may seem an intolerable burden. But when one has become accustomed to the practice it is impossible not to realize how much of the feeling of intense participation always felt in an Orthodox liturgy is due to it. A seated assembly is almost necessarily a passive assembly. And it is not disposed by its position to worship but at best to accept some instruction, or most of the time just to look more or less curiously at a spectacle in which it takes no part. Even when it kneels to pray it will be for a private prayer and not for a common supplication. And just as a sitting assembly usually sings badly or not at all, it is hopeless to try to bring it together to praise and thanksgiving.

If we cannot now suppress the seats altogether in our churches, we should certainly make them a much secondary feature, first by reducing them to light movable chairs. Today especially when chairs of light metallic material can be made in such a way that they may be noiselessly moved, and even folded and removed when not in use, this is extremely easy. It will mean for the building and furnishing of a church a substantial saving which will afford greater opportunities of money to be spent in things more important in a church. These movable chairs will make it possible, in celebrations with youngsters, to dispense with the chairs, and maybe in the future to reintroduce progressively the older and far better use of standing congregations.

Immediately it will make it easier for any congregation to become a real congregation, whatever the number of people meeting in the same church; and, what is essential, it will again be possible to have general movements and that progression without which there is no community between the faithful, or only a kind of petrified community.

For to have a satisfactory celebration of the eucharist it is essential that the congregation be able to group in different ways and move freely from one to the other.

For the service of readings and prayers one of the best dispositions might be approximately circular, centered on the pulpit or lectern where the readings and the homily are given, with the celebrant himself seated on a platform at a short distance, facing the reader. Better still the gathering should be in the shape of an ellipse, not too lengthy, with the lectern and the seat at both focuses of the ellipse on a single *Bema*. This does not need a building of that shape but could be achieved as well in a square or oblong building. If oblong it should not be more extended in its length than twice its breadth. If this proportion is not observed the homogeneity of the gathering will be lost and the unity of the choral singing slackened. The choristers in any case should find room between the seat of the celebrant and the lectern.

Another disposition could be inspired

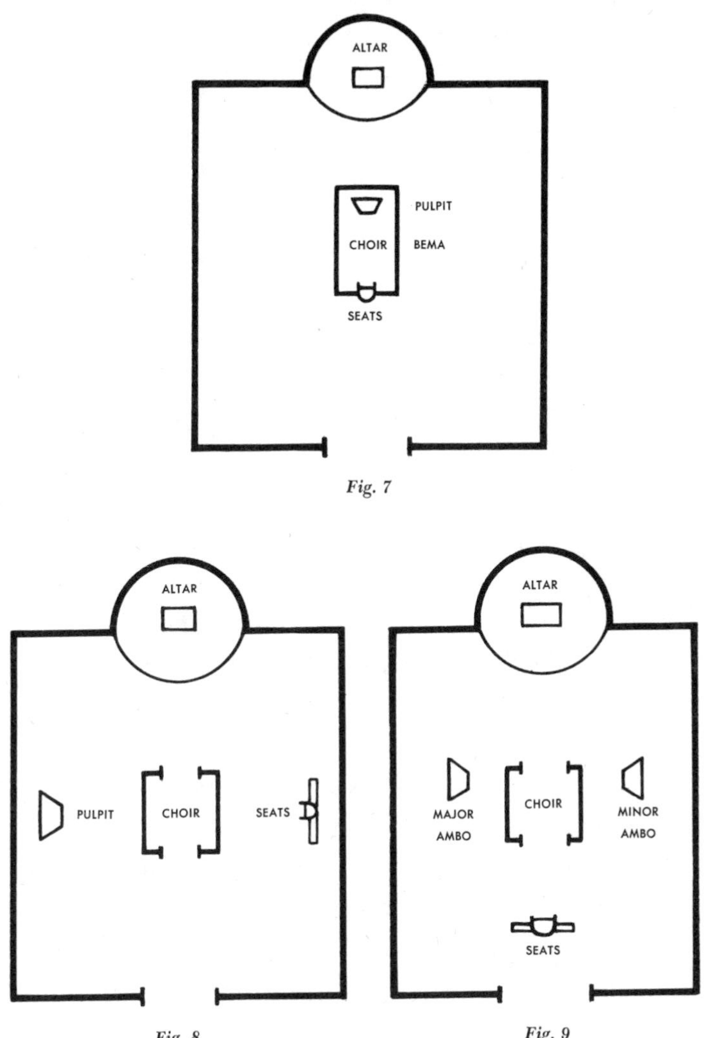

Figs. 7, 8, and 9. Ideal arrangements suggested for modern churches, with choir located in the very middle of the church, not necessarily raised on one or more steps. An approximately square building with an apse is depicted, but various forms—elliptic, circular, or triangular—could be adapted to the same basic idea. (See also Figs. 10 and 11.)

by the late mediaeval pulpit and "banc d'oeuvre." The pulpit would be on one side (the so-called Gospel side), the celebrant being seated in front of it and the choir again between them in the center. A third disposition could be with the seat of the celebrant near the entrance or, whatever may be the disposition of the doors, opposite the altar, with either one pulpit about at the center or two ambos on either side as in the Roman basilicas.

The pulpit or ambos, especially, when there are more than one, the higher ambo, should be more than an ordinary lectern. It must be made clear by its dimensions and design that it is the most sacred place in the church after the altar itself. It could be combined for this with some re-invented form of the ark, either as a small house or cupboard, or as an armary or aumbry in the wall with a veil like the canopy of the tabernacle and lights. To have a seven-branched candlestick near the ark together with seven lamps around the altar (as in the vision of the Apocalypse) would emphasize the connection between these two focuses of the celebration.

Even if no restoration of the ark is attempted, the ambo of the Gospel at least should be always wide enough to admit not only the priest or deacon but also the candle-bearers and the incense-bearer. One massive candlestick, as in the Roman basilicas (or two, one on each side) should underline the fact that the presence of Christ is made manifest where His word is announced, before He comes within us at the altar. When, as is much to be desired, the pulpit or ambo is near the center of the church, some representation above it, on the wall, the ceiling or a cupola, of the risen Christ having the Gospel in His hand would be also very meaningful.

We may encourage the practice of associating laymen duly prepared for this to the celebration by giving them the epistle or the Old Testament lesson to read. In that case they, as well as the chief cantors should always wear a liturgical dress: alb or surplice, and in case of a more solemn celebration the cope. Such a garment is not to be regarded as a typically clerical dress but, like the white garment of the newly baptized, as the festal decking of the kingly priesthood common to all the believers.

If one insists on keeping some chancel near the altar, there could be a single pulpit on the North side at the entrance or at a small

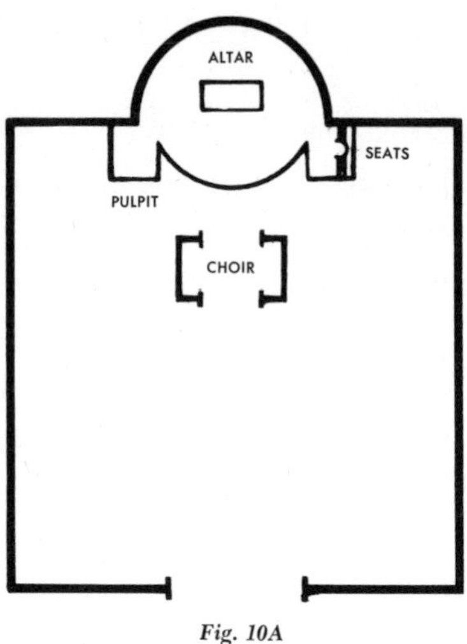

Fig. 10A

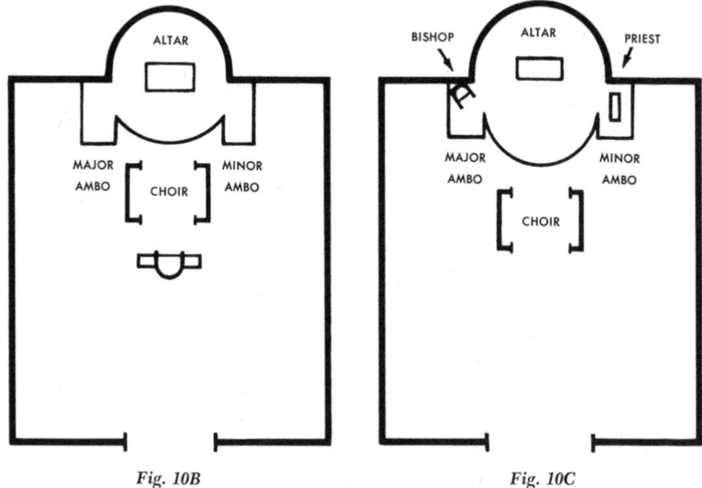

Fig. 10B

Fig. 10C

Fig. 10. Further possibilities of choir arrangements. These may even be reconciled with the use of pews.

distance of the entrance of that chancel. The seat of the celebrant, then should face it on the other side. Or two ambos could be used either with the seat of the celebrant between them in the middle of the first ranks of the faithful, or combined with the lower ambo if the celebrant is not the bishop himself, or with the higher if the bishop celebrates. In all these cases the choir should be in the first ranks of the faithful rather than in the chancel itself.

These last possibilities (and also that of a church with the seat of the celebrant at the extreme opposite to the altar) could be reconciled with the use of pews. However, the more the whole celebration is concentrated from the beginning to the end in the same part of the building, and the less the actual introduction of the faithful into the celebration is felt, the less also the progression of the office becomes sensible.

For any prayer the celebrant, whatever his position at the moment, should always turn toward the faithful to invite them to pray, and then toward the altar together with the whole congregation for the prayer itself. For the prayer of the faithful after the homily the high ambo or pulpit should be used by the deacon or a priest other than the main celebrant, turning also to the congregation for the monitions giving the themes of the prayer, but toward the altar for the prayer itself.

It should be noted here that the *oratio fidelium* is properly a prayer *of the faithful themselves,* not of the priest or the deacon for them, even associating them to it by soliciting a response. Its original form, as we find it still in the *Orationes solemnes* of Good Friday, is made of an invitation to prayer by the celebrant, a monition (preferably by the deacon) on the object of prayer, then a moment of silent prayer during which everyone of the faithful is supposed to pray personally for the intention proposed, and only after that a collect in which the celebrant very briefly summarizes the prayers of all. Then they give their Amen.

It is after the readings, the chants of meditation between them sung by the cantors (except the acclamation of the alleluia which should be taken up by all), the homily and these prayers that the celebrant is to move to the altar. He should be followed there by a first procession of all the faithful with general singing or alternate singing between the choir and all, to bring the gifts of all at the altar itself. When this, owing to a great number of participants, cannot conveniently be done, the procession of the celebrant and his ministers should be followed at least by a procession of some representative members of the whole community bringing the bread and wine to the altar, maybe with the offering of money collected quickly at this time. The celebrant having received the gifts would ascend the steps of the altar, the collectors standing at the foot at least until the sacrifice is ready to be consecrated and the great incensation has begun.

This brings us to the problem of the disposition of the altar.

The Roman instruction given for a first application of the Conciliar Constitution on the liturgy insists on the fact that the whole church has to be centered on the altar, while in churches newly built or restored it should be at least at some distance from the wall, so that celebration *versus populum* may be possible. These few words combined with the TV transmission of the first concelebrated masses under the presidence of the pope at Saint Peter's during the Council have been enough to create the impression in many minds that most or all of the liturgical renewal depends on having the mass "facing the people." What we have said before should be enough to dissipate the illusion.

Certainly such a celebration is and has always been perfectly regular in all the churches using the Roman liturgy, supported as it is by a long practice of the Roman basilicas. The fact that the altar is a table, on the other hand, and as such should never be put just against the wall is nothing new in the liturgical laws of the West as of the East. Not only in the *Ceremoniale episcoporum,* but as well in the much older *Pontificale romanum,* in the way in which is described the consecration of the major altar of a church, it had always been made perfectly clear. And, as the instruction puts it, when this old prescription is obeyed, as it should have been always, the celebration *versus populum* if wanted is possible. But the instruction never says or implies in any way that it is necessarily everywhere and always the best possible form of celebration.

It is true that some of the pioneers of the liturgical movement some fifty years ago, especially Dom Lambert Beauduin, the monk of Mont-César, encouraged in some measure that practice which had been always in the modern rubrics but not used outside of a few churches in Rome. But the question is why did they do that?

Having been one of the first to promote it in my country, I am rather well aware of the motives; they were mainly three. The first and foremost was that at the time, especially for a mass said or sung by a single priest without deacon or subdeacon, the rubrics enforced the reading of the biblical texts not only from the altar, but from a book placed on the altar itself. The attempt, therefore, to restore the full significance of that first part of the mass needed a disposition of the altar such that the readings may become again a reality. They were evidently to remain meaningless, a mere dead formality, as long as they were made by a reader turning his back to the audience. The celebration "facing the people" was an easy, and the only possible, solution at the time. However, now that the Instruction mentioned has restored, with the practice of reading the Bible in the vernacular, that of having it read always from a lectern or ambo, that basic justification in modern times of the celebration "facing the people" has disappeared.

A second motive was the necessity of restoring the fundamental view of the mass as being a meal as well as a sacrifice. Then since, in modern times, we have become accustomed to take our meals in our homes around the family table, using the altar in such a way could become a pedagogical device to reawaken the basic sense of the eucharist as the community meal of the people of God.

However, this itself could not and can never be achieved except if the people are really gathered *around* the table and not just standing before it with the celebrant alone on the other side. Nothing, of course, can be more foreign to any real meal than this. Therefore, from the first, the pioneers of the liturgical movement have been insisting that the celebration *versus populum* is not a panacea and that, indeed, it can have good effects only when practised in such a way as to make the gathering of all around the altar a reality. This is still valid and that is to say that it may be very good particularly in the case of a rather small community, and especially with groups of people who are to be taught the communal character of the mass.

But men like Dom Lambert Beauduin and his first followers were too good scholars ever to try to defend the practice on the chimerical ground that it should be considered the primitive one. They knew perfectly well that it was not. They just advocated it as providing us with opportunities for a quite new situation and for pedagogical adaptations, while being in perfect conformity with the rubrics of the time.

What must also be frankly avowed is that Dom Lambert Beauduin and his disciples, because of their insistence on restoring the reading of the Bible to its primitive place in the mass and their describing the mass as a community meal in which all had to participate, were constantly accused of being just Protestants in disguise. Therefore they insisted also on the fact that in celebrating the mass in such a way, far from leaning toward Protestantism, they were only going back to an old Roman use and were, if it may be said, only more Roman than the Romans themselves.

Fortunately, this innocent caption has now lost its object. It has finally come to be acknowledged by everyone, at least in principle, that the biblical character of the first part of the mass has to be restored as a true service of the word, while the eucharistic sacrifice itself has to be performed in a communal meal in which all are to participate. To do that we no longer need the artificial cover of a local use of the Church of Rome. It has now been proclaimed in a most solemn way by an Ecumenical Council as the official tradition of the whole Catholic Church. Therefore, it is clear that the question of celebrating in front of or behind the altar is not to be seen as a matter of principle but just as a matter of expediency. It depends on the circumstances and whether they can be used better in one or the other way. Two of the major motives which could justify the insistence on a forgotten mode in the former generation have disappeared altogether. The only one still extant, the paedagogical aspect, is not now so strong as it was some years ago, the principle that the mass *is* a community meal having become accepted everywhere. This motive will come into play, then, only when the circumstances of the celebration will be such that they will favor the pedagogical use of the altar facing the people, and insofar as such a pedagogy may be still needed. This is far from being the more general case.

Every time the altar facing the people means just an altar with the priest alone (and maybe his ministers) on one side and the people on the other side, it will have only the opposite effect, as it is growingly felt by the people themselves. Far from uniting the community focused on the altar, it will emphasize the separation and opposition between clergy and laity; the altar will just become itself the most formidable barrier between two castes among the Christians. Far from creating a greater participation of all, it will develop still more the most baleful bequest of the middle ages: the wrong idea that the liturgy is something that the clergy, as a body of privileged specialists, are to do for the benefit of the others, and not something to be done *with* the people, the clergy only heading them in the common celebration.

In most cases therefore, especially in the average parochial church, from the very point of view of restoring a true common celebration, it must be said frankly that the priest standing on the same side as the people for the eucharistic prayer as the visible leader of their whole body remains the better practice. What is only needed, then, is that there might be as little breach as possible between the priest, the ministers and the whole congregation. It means that the altar should never be lost in some inaccessible sanctuary but always at a short distance of the first ranks of the people. What is needed especially is, for the offering and the communion, that they may come as near to it as possible. This will be best achieved by a disposition of the congregation which will make it at the time of the eucharistic prayer gathered in a more or less semi-circular way behind the celebrant.

Neither should it be forgotten that a completely circular gathering at this moment, even if it can help people of today at first to realize the communal character of the eucharist, which is only the case when there is just one rank or very few ranks of participants, is never the ideal one. Once again the ideal of the church is not that of a human family closed upon itself. It could be even questioned whether this could ever be the ideal of a really healthy family. The Christian family must always be open, open to the invisible Church of all the other Christians in this world or the next, open to the world and beyond the world to the eternal kingdom.

This means also that the altar facing the people, in the case of a great assembly, will be really successful only when it is not at the chord of the apse, as in the medieval disposition of the Roman basilica, but in the nave

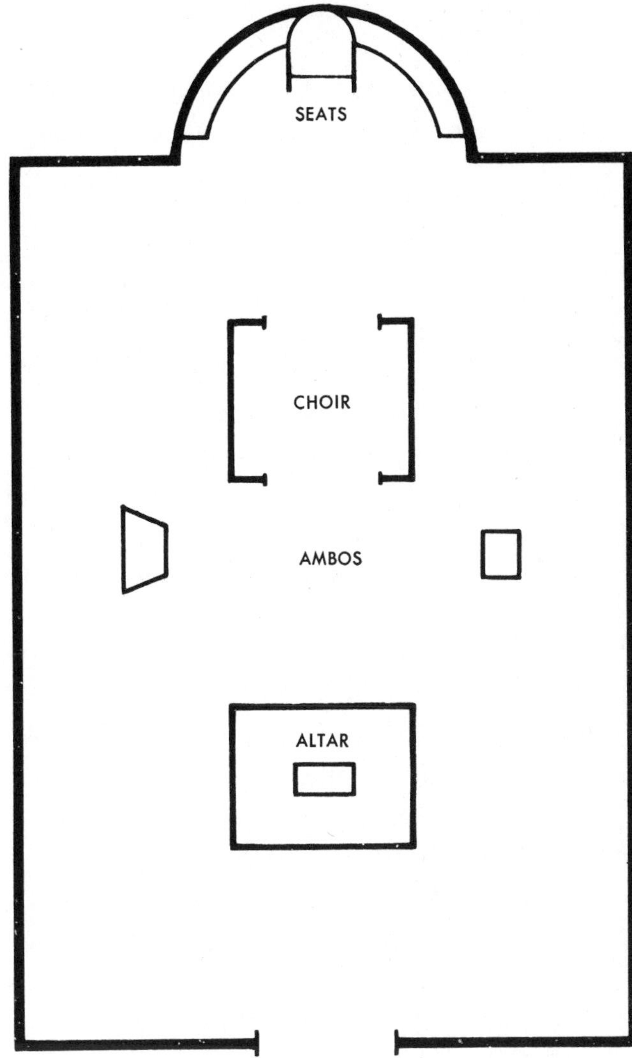

Fig. 11. Altar facing the people located in the nave of the church. Such an arrangement would have the great central door, as in the very early synagogue, open beyond the altar, and the advantage of contiguity between clergy and people.

itself. Thus only will there be not just the clergy on one side, but a part at least of the congregation together with them, and the other part on the other side (or rather sides) of the altar while, as in the more ancient use of the basilica by the synagogue, the great central door of the church will open beyond it. Such a disposition can have great dignity, and if the continuity remains unbroken between clergy and people it may have the advantage, especially in great cathedrals, of leaving nobody too far from the altar. But generally, even in this rather exceptional case of a celebration with a great concourse of people, it may well be wondered whether a better disposition was not that which had been kept in Rome itself until the time of Pascal I, which left the bishop in the midst of his people, not so much above them but rather as the heart of the body.

This brings us in conclusion to a few remarks concerning the altar and its ornamentation. The altar is a table but it is not any kind of table, just as the eucharist is a meal but not any kind of meal. It is a festive table and the table of a sacred meal, a sacrificial meal. Therefore a just attachment to evangelical poverty should not lead us to think as it seems to be the case now with many priests that the ideal table should be a kitchen table. Evangelical poverty means that we should always think of the poor first and never spend for our egotistical needs what could be saved for their necessities. This may mean in times of need that a local church will have to sell its most costly sacred furnitures; it may mean also that it should spend weekly more for the poor than for the necessities of worship. But it can never mean that of all things in the church the altar could ever be something meaner than the furnitures all of us use in our homes. By its situation, its shape and proportions, its material and working, the altar should always be the most beautified object in the church. It may be such while remaining simple, especially if the ancient use of clothing it with varied antependiums is maintained as it should be. It must be raised on some steps (always more than the seat of the celebrant, even of the bishop), but especially in a church of moderate dimensions never so as to give an impression of remoteness.

It is a most ancient and most fitting decoration of the altar that connects lights with it. Hanging lamps should always accompany the main altar, even if the Blessed sacrament is not reserved upon it. For the celebration, the mediaeval use of putting two candlesticks on its table at each extremity is very dignified and should not be abandoned lightly. But from purely esthetic motives as well as because the altar is not a support for any kind of secondary objects more than this number should be avoided. Two or four great candlesticks added on each side at some distance from the altar or at the four extremities of the platform where it stands are certainly much better for a more solemn celebration.

On the other hand, even when the mass is not celebrated facing the people, the presence of the sacrament in a tabernacle at the altar of the public celebration is neither ancient nor the ideal. If or when the sacrament cannot be kept in a separate chapel, the best seems to return to the practice of the aumbry in the wall of the sanctuary. But especially if the altar is used facing the people it is better that the aumbry be on the north side of the altar (the so-called Gospel side). It could be a good practice, in small churches at least, to have the aumbry of the sacrament on one side and the ark of scriptures on the other side.

The presence of an image of the cross with

the crucifix, even if it was not always at the altar in Christian antiquity, is one of these very old although not exactly primitive traditions which have become universal and should be always retained. The connection between the cross and the mass will never be too strongly emphasized. There is no necessity of having the crucifix on the altar itself. In the case of the celebration facing the people and in other cases a great crucifix hanging from the ceiling above the altar, or raised on a triumphal arch either above or before it, or painted on the wall behind, is often to be preferred. The beam of the English "rood" or French "tref," with the crucifix between lamps or tapers, was in the small church of the mediaeval era an adaptation of the pulpitum of the cathedrals. It could be revived by the modern architects as an excellent way of enhancing the sacred character of the holy table without crowding it with objects not strictly necessary to the celebration.

But the decoration of the wall behind the altar or the cupola above it, either through mosaics, painting, tapestry or stained glass, should always add to the cross some evocation of that cosmic and supra-cosmic vision of faith which makes of the eucharist a foretaste of the transfiguration of the whole world in the coming of the kingdom.

The vestments of the celebrant and his ministers should always be designed to fit with the altar and its surroundings, as in the fine chapel of the convent of Dominican sisters at Vence (France) by Matisse. They are not to be considered so much as personal insignia (in the old Roman Church all the officiants from the pope to the last acolyte wore the same paenula) but rather as the nuptial garment with which the Church is to make her entrance into the banquet hall of her heavenly Spouse. They should help the faithful to realize the festal character of every eucharistic celebration when, as Saint Augustine has expressed it in unforgettable words, we are, having a first glimpse of the eternal Temple, to be transported into it from the tabernacles of our temporal pilgrimage, our voices echoing the unceasing praise of the holy and ever living God.

The colors of the vestments as well as of the altar hangings should recover the full variety of the mediaeval tradition, when the penitential character of Lent was underlined by the grey clothing of both the altar and the officiants (or even the use of a plain kind of sackcloth, the so-called "Lenten array"), while the great festivals were a constantly renewed feast of colour, with the white for the feasts of Our Lord and of the virgins, the blue for those of the Mother of God, the red for the martyrs and all the Sundays after Pentecost, the yellow for the confessors, the purple for Septuagesima and Advent, the pink for the weeks of Gaudete and Laetare, and the green for the time after Epiphany.[13]

A simple but always perfectly ordered ceremonial, with abundant and varied singing, incense and lights, in a church exactly and beautifully adapted to its purpose, is a powerful help to a realization of the spiritual joy without which there is certainly no genuine eucharistic worship. Our purely rubrical modern conception of the liturgy, our dull didacticism, our abstract spirituality, on the other hand, go together with the uninspired buildings where we perform a sullen "Sunday duty." All that will have to disappear if we are ever again to be on earth some real anticipation of "the Church of the firstborn, whose names are inscribed in heaven."

[13] This is an example of the way in which the different colours could be used, still at the end of the middle ages, but there were many local variations.

Once again, to conclude, none of the details we have examined, taken either in isolation or all together, will be able to restore to us a living worship. It is a matter of a fully renewed spirit. But the Christian spirit means nothing as long as we do not realize it has to be embodied to be real. The embodiment of the spirit of worship is a Christian church worthy of the title. The concrete suggestions we have been able to formulate must only be considered as a few samples of the unlimited possibilities open to architects by tradition rightly understood, as both an undying source of inspiration and a challenge to creative freedom.

APPENDIX I: CONCELEBRATION

We have said nothing of concelebration because as soon as a church is disposed as it should be it becomes very easy everywhere. We must remember that in a parochial church concelebration will be a rare occurrence, just because the normal parochial worship is the worship of the local congregation around its pastor. What is needed for concelebration is what is needed for any good celebration of the pastor with his folk: an altar easy of access with nothing useless around it. Especially important is to have a wide place immediately at the foot of the altar where the communicants can be grouped together to receive communion together, as many as there may be. "Stations," as they are called, where communicants receive individually from individual clergy are just as bad as simultaneous individual celebrations by individual priests at the same time in the same church.

APPENDIX II: THE BAPTISTRY

We have said nothing of the baptistry, because its place is neither the church nor in the church. Baptism is a rite of entrance, the conclusion of which should be the first introduction into the eucharistic community. Therefore, the baptistry should be either a separate building near the entrance of the church or situated in a distinct atrium leading to the church. Even if there is little hope in the near future of restoring the baptism of adults to the importance it should always have in a missionary Church (which any church should always be), the baptistry must never be reduced to a place for the fount of infant baptism. This fount itself should become again a true bath where baptism by immersion (the most normal and traditional form, still kept today by the Orthodox, as it was kept in many countries of Europe until the beginning of this century) might be at least possible. Moreover it should be situated at the centre of an excavation with a sufficient depth to restore the fundamental symbolism of being buried in water, to rise again to the life of the Spirit. The decoration of the room here as in the church itself should be fully expressive of the meaning of the ritual.[14]

When in the atrium of the church, the baptistry could easily be combined with the stoups of holy water from which the faithful are to sprinkle themselves again every time they come to mass.

Similarly the confessionals, where the right of access to the eucharist when lost is to be restored, should be also either in the atrium or near the actual entrance of the church.

[14] Cf. F. Dölger, "Zur Symbolik des altchristlichen Taufhauses," *Antike und Christentum,* IV, 1934, pp. 153 ff.; L. de Bruyne, "La decoration des baptisteres paleochretiens," *Miscellanea Liturgica in Honorem L. C. Mohlberg,* I, Rome, 1948, pp. 189 ff.

INDEX

altar,
in Byzantine churches, 62–63
in Constantinian basilicas, 45, 46, 48, 50
disposition of the, 105–106, 111–112
"facing the people," 51ff., 82–83, 105, 106, 107ff.
ornamentation of the, 114–118
significance of, 31
architecture,
churches and, 92–94
liturgy and, 5–6, 92–93
see also churches
Ark,
found in synagogues, 14–15, 19
in primitive churches, 33, 45–46, 62
significance of the original Ark, 11–14
atrium, 41
aumbry, 116
baptistry, 121–122
basilica,

Constantinian, 43ff.
modification of the primitive Roman, 50ff.
on the origin of the Roman, 39ff.
used as synagogue, 17–19
bema, 16, 27, 34, 38–39, 45–46, 62, 65, 71
Byzantine churches,
architectural characteristics of, 60–62
iconography in, 66, 68–69
reading of Scripture in, 65–66
cartibulum, 41
chancel, 51, 79–80, 101, 103
churches,
circular, 93
desirable architectural features, 92–94
dispositions for the reading of Scripture in, 98–101
function of, 6, 7–8
modern, 6–7
in North Africa, 42–43
orientation of, 94–96
Roman, *see* basilica
seats in, 96–98
symbolism of geographical orientation of, 28–30
synagogue and, 8–9
see also architecture
concelebration, 120–121
eucharist,
celebration of the eucharist in patristic times, 56–60
communion of the faithful, 49
keeping of the, 84–86
as real presence, 30–31

as sacrifice, 32, 33, 48, 49–50, 109, 110
vestments in the celebration of the, 118–119
Holy of holies, *see* Ark
iconography,
in Byzantine churches, 66, 68–69
origin of, 66–68
impluvium, 41
liturgical renewal, meaning of, 1–2, 105–106
liturgy,
architecture and, 5–6, 92–93
definition of, 3, 4–5
participation of the congregation in, 101, 103–105, 110, 111–114
tradition and, 3–4, 86–87
see also worship
martyr, cult of, 48
ministers,
function of ministers in Christian worship, 89–92
in primitive churches, 35–36, 45
padigliano, 46–48
prone, 75–76
pulpitum, 74, 75, 76, 100
reredo, 77–79
schola, 46
seat of Moses, 10–11, 16–17, 32, 33
Shekinah, 13–14, 30
solea, 65
synagogue,
basilicas used as, 17
function of, 9–10, 15–16, 19–20
iconography in, 67–68
prototype of the church, 8–9

reading of Scripture in, 15–16, 19
Syrian church and, 25ff.
worship in the, 10, 19, 21–24, 35, 36–38
Syrian churches,
altar in, 31
differences from synagogues, 27–28
function of the minister in, 35–36
liturgical services in, 34–36
reading of Scripture in, 32
similarities with synagogues, 25–27
throne,
in Byzantine churches, 65
in Constantinian churches, 43, 46
in Roman basilicas, 52
in Syrian churches, 33–34
tradition,
liturgy and, 3–4, 86–87
as a source of Christian life, 3
tendencies toward, 2–3
triclinium, 41
Western churches,
development of, 70–71, 74, 79–80
influence exerted or absorbed by, 83–84
reading of Scripture in, 75–76
seating of the congregation in, 80
women,
participation in Christian worship, 38–39, 62
participation in synagogal worship, 37–38
worship,
in Byzantine churches, 61–62, 63
in catacombs, 40
function and meaning of Christian worship, 87, 88–89, 92, 119–120

in the medieval period, 63–65
participation of the congregation, 101, 103–105, 110, 111–114
in primitive churches, 35–36, 38–39, 45, 49–50
seating or standing during worship, 96–98
synagogal, 21–22, 23, 37–38, 87–88
in Western churches, 71–72, 81–82